DEVELOPMENTAL SCHOOL COUNSELING PROGRAMS: FROM THEORY TO PRACTICE

Pamela O. Paisley, EdD
Glenda T. Hubbard, PhD

Developmental School Counseling Programs

Copyright © 1994 by the American Counseling Association. All rights reserved. Printed in the United States of America. Except as permitted under the United States Copyright Act of 1976, no part of this publication may be reproduced or distributed in any form or by any means, or stored in a database or retrieval system, without the prior written permission of the publisher.

10 9 8 7 6 5 4 3 2 1

American Counseling Association
5999 Stevenson Avenue
Alexandria, VA 22304

Director of Communications
Jennifer L. Sacks

Acquisitions and Development Editor
Carolyn Baker

Production/Design Manager
Michael Comlish

Copyeditor
Heather Jefferson

Cover design by Martha Woolsey

Library of Congress Cataloging-in-Publication Data

Paisley, Pamela O.
    Developmental school counseling programs: from theory to practice / Pamela O. Paisley, Glenda T. Hubbard.
       p. cm.
    Includes bibliographical references.
    ISBN 1-55620-139-7
    1. Educational counseling—United States. 2. Student assistance programs—United States. 3. Child psychology—United States. I. Hubbard, Glenda T. II. Title.
LB1027.5.P276   1994
371.4'0973—dc20
                                                               94-850
                                                                      CIP

*To the children, adolescents, graduate students, and
school counselors who have taught us much*

*Watch me. I'm making a cocoon.
It looks like I'm hiding, I know,
but a cocoon is no escape.
It's an in-between house where
the change takes place.
It's a big step since you can
never return to caterpillar life.
During the change, it will seem
to you or to anyone who might
peek that nothing is happening—
but the butterfly is already becoming.
It just takes time.*

—from *Hope for the Flowers* by Trina Paulus (NY: Paulist Press, 1972)

TABLE OF CONTENTS

Preface xi
Acknowledgments xiii
About the Authors xv
Introduction xvii

PART ONE
DEVELOPMENTAL THEORY: CONCEPTS AND IMPACT ON SCHOOL COUNSELING PROGRAMS

CHAPTER 1: Concepts and Use of Developmental Theories .. 3
   Domains of Development............................. 3
      Cognitive Development 3
      Ethical Reasoning 5
      Conceptual Level 7
      Psychosocial Development 8
      Interpersonal Development 10
      Career Development 10
      Developmental Tasks 13

   How Development Occurs............................. 14
      Mechanisms of Change 14
      Developmental Assumptions 14

   Promoting Development 15
      Components of Successful Programs 15
      Dilemma Discussions 16
      Plus-One Reasoning 17
      Significant Role-Taking Experiences 17
      Person–Environment Fit 18

   Summary 18

TABLE OF CONTENTS

CHAPTER 2: The Impact of Developmental Theory on Individual Counseling 21

Relationship Building 21
    Characteristics of a Helping Relationship 22
    Stages of a Helping Relationship 22
    Roadblocks to Effective Communication 23

Assessment.. 24

Strategies... 26
    Play Media and Expressive Arts................... 26
    Gestalt Approaches 27
    Systematic Problem Solving...................... 28
    Behavioral Contracts 28
    Cognitive–Behavioral Approaches 29

Summary... 30

CHAPTER 3: The Impact of Developmental Theory on Group Counseling 31

Topics and Competencies........................... 32
Classroom Interventions or Small Groups 34
Choice of Materials 36
Scheduling....................................... 37
Components from Successful Programs to
    Promote Development 38
ASCA Materials 40

Summary... 40

CHAPTER 4: Working with Parents and Teachers 43

Sharing Developmental Information 43

Adult Development 44

A Specific Application 45
    Counselor-Led Support Groups 47
    The First Session 48
    Succeeding Sessions............................. 48
    Guided Reflection 49
    Potential Benefits............................... 49

Summary... 50

References for Part One 51

PART TWO
SAMPLE DEVELOPMENTAL PROGRAMS

INTRODUCTION TO PART TWO 55

CHAPTER 5: *The Role of Moral Development in Deciding How to Counsel Children and Adolescents* by Gerald D. Parr and Mary Ostrovsky 57

    Stages of Moral Development 58
        Preconventional Level 59
        Conventional Level 59
        Postconventional, Autonomous, or Principled Level 59

    Moral Stages and Counseling Strategies................ 60
        Preconventional Level 60
        Conventional Level 62

    Conclusions 64

    References 65

CHAPTER 6: *Children's Literature as a Resource for Classroom Guidance* by Sarah Borders and Pamela O. Paisley 67

    Method 68
        Participants 68
        Procedures 69
        Instruments 69

    The Intervention 70

    Results... 72

    Discussion 73

    Implications...................................... 74

    References 75

    Additional Resources 77

TABLE OF CONTENTS

CHAPTER 7: *Peer Counseling for Middle School Students Experiencing Family Divorce: A Deliberate Psychological Education Model*
by Norman A. Sprinthall, Janice S. Hall, and Edwin R. Gerler, Jr. 79

Peer Counseling: An Untapped Resource 80
   Directing Constructs 80

Research Design 82
   Experimental Groups 82
   Measures 83
   The Educational Intervention 83

Results 84
   Statistical Analysis 85
   Qualitative Results 87

Discussion 87

References 90

Appendix A 93

Appendix B 96

CHAPTER 8: *The Dilemma in Drug Abuse Prevention*
by Robert Paisley, Edwin R. Gerler, Jr., and Norman A. Sprinthall 101

Method 102
   Participants 102
   Procedure 103

Results 107
   Changes in Principled Reasoning 107
   Changes in Conceptual Level 109

Discussion 110

Conclusion 111

References 112

PART THREE
SAMPLE DEVELOPMENTAL LESSON PLANS

INTRODUCTION TO PART THREE 117

CHAPTER 9: School Success 119
    Introduction 119
    Goals 119
    Sample Objectives 120
    Sample Lesson Plans 121

CHAPTER 10: Effective Problem Solving 133
    Introduction 133
    Goals 134
    Sample Objectives 134
    Sample Lesson Plans 136

CHAPTER 11: Identity Formation 147
    Introduction 147
    Goals 148
    Sample Objectives 148
    Sample Lesson Plans 149

CHAPTER 12: Respect for Self and Others 159
    Introduction 159
    Goals 159
    Sample Objectives 160
    Sample Lesson Plans 161

TABLE OF CONTENTS

CHAPTER 13: Wellness 173
    Introduction 173
    Goals 174
    Sample Objectives 175
    Sample Lesson Plans 176

CHAPTER 14: Changes 193
    Introduction 193
    Goals 194
    Sample Objectives 194
    Sample Lesson Plans 195

PART FOUR
SAMPLE K–12 GOALS AND COMPETENCIES

INTRODUCTION TO PART FOUR 207
    Mission 207
    Philosophy 208
    Domains 208

CHAPTER 15: Sample Goals and Competencies 209
    Personal-Social Domain 209
        Goals 209
        Competencies 209
    Educational Domain 214
        Goals 214
        Competencies 214
    Career Domain 218
        Goals 218
        Competencies 218
    References for Part Four 221

Preface

This book is intended to offer assistance in translating developmental theory to practice. Although primarily focused for school counselors, this text could also be beneficial to school psychologists, social workers, parents, and teachers interested in learning more about development and how to promote it.

Part One addresses developmental theories and their impact on school counseling programs. Chapter 1 includes an overview of several domains of development and a presentation of methods of promoting development. Chapters 2 and 3 examine the impact of this developmental framework on individual and group counseling, respectively. Chapter 4 presents ideas for using developmental theory in working with teachers and parents. This chapter also provides an outline for a specific intervention with first-year teachers.

The chapters in Part Two are reprinted journal articles from *The School Counselor* and *Elementary School Guidance and Counseling*. They are designed to provide sample programs based on the developmental principles covered in Part One. Chapter 5 outlines specific strategies and approaches for use in individual counseling developed by Parr and Ostrovsky, which are based on stages of moral reasoning. Chapters 6–8 describe successful group interventions designed to promote development. A sample program is provided for elementary, middle school, and high school settings. At the elementary level, a classroom intervention using quality children's literature is described by Borders and Paisley. A peer counseling program for middle school students experiencing divorce is presented by Sprinthall, Hall, and Gerler. An intervention using dilemma discussion with high school students to prevent drug abuse is outlined by Paisley, Gerler, and Sprinthall.

Part Three provides sample developmental lesson plans in six topical areas: (a) school success, (b) effective problem solving, (c) identity formation, (d) respect for self and others, (e) wellness, and (f) dealing with change. These lessons are intended to be used as part of complete developmental programs that use what we know from stage theory and from previous successful interventions. Such programs are ongoing and provide the appropriate balance of challenge, support, and reflection over time.

Part Four provides an additional approach to developmental and proactive programming by offering K–12 goals and competencies in three domains. These domains are personal/social, educational, and career-vocational. This approach represents a system-wide program and is expanded from a K–8 program designed by the elementary counselors in the Watauga County School System in Boone, North Carolina.

Throughout the book, an emphasis is placed on the counseling program being an integral part of the total learning experience. Counselors are encouraged to: (a) write clear goals and objectives, (b) share these with school personnel and parents, and (c) assess outcomes of interventions. Awareness of developmental characteristics will assist counselors in adapting the length, style, and vocabulary for various developmental levels. Knowledge concerning the methods of promoting development suggests specific strategies that would attract students to the next stage.

Most significantly, the emphasis of the book is that developmental school counseling programs can (and, in fact, must) have a strong theoretical foundation. Such programs reflect a philosophy and a commitment to serving the whole child and to educational and preventive programming.

Acknowledgments

The authors would like to thank numerous individuals who have contributed their personal and/or professional support to this project: the graduate students and the practicing school counselors with whom we have had the pleasure of working through the years; our department chair, Dr. Lee Baruth; the faculty and staff within our own department at Appalachian; our larger circle of colleagues in counselor education who share our commitment to school counseling; Watauga County Schools and their counselors for allowing us to expand on their system-wide program in Part Four; our editor at ACA, Carolyn Baker; our reviewers, Dr. Ed Gerler and Dr. Norman Sprinthall; and our families and friends for putting up with the book-writing process.

Special thanks to Tonya Barlow, Terri Kearse, Leslie Rainey, Lisa Murray, Ann Marie Rice, Anna Suddreth, Kathy Simmons, Sarah Borders, and Patricia Maynard for their individual, and in some cases numerous, contributions to the manuscript.

About the Authors

Pam Paisley worked as a teacher and a counselor in public schools for 10 years prior to entering counselor education. She has worked as a school counselor in elementary, middle school, and high school settings. Her doctorate focused on developmental theory and is from North Carolina State University in Raleigh. She has been a member of the School Counseling Program faculty within the Department of Human Development and Psychological Counseling at Appalachian State University for 7 years. Dr. Paisley is active in professional associations at the state, regional, and national levels, currently chairing the Association for Counselor Education and Supervision (ACES) School Counseling Interest Network.

Glenda Hubbard has a long history of commitment to the promotion of the school counseling profession. After serving as a school counselor in Miami, Florida, for 7 years, she became a counselor educator at Appalachian State University, where she has taught for 19 years. Dr. Hubbard currently coordinates the School Counseling Program. She has been involved in leadership roles in the North Carolina Counseling Association and the North Carolina School Counselor Association for a number of years, and has been a member of American School Counselors Association (ASCA) since 1965. She holds a PhD from the University of Miami in Coral Gables, Florida.

Introduction

Children and adolescents within American society face many challenges. As adults interested in helping children, we only have to look at the statistics concerning substance abuse, divorce, poverty, violence, dropouts, or teen pregnancy to realize that these challenges have reached critical proportions. Additionally, many children and adolescents who may not become statistics may also not reach their full potential (Glosoff & Kopowicz, 1990), falling through the cracks of a system relying heavily on crisis intervention.

What can be done? One approach that shows great promise is to focus on promoting healthy development, rather than waiting for problems to occur. Children and adolescents who have positive self-concepts, effective communication and decision-making skills, good peer relations, and strong egos are unlikely to be as vulnerable to society's ills. For any adults interested in assisting young people, this approach has special meaning. We must understand what development is and how it occurs. Regardless of whether our interest is personal or professional, we must advocate for the implementation of programs and interventions that proactively promote development, rather than reactively responding to problems.

For school counselors, this means the implementation of comprehensive developmental school counseling programs. Encouragement for these types of programs comes from: (a) the literature (Gysbers & Henderson, 1994; Myrick, 1987), (b) position statements of professional associations (American School Counselor Association, 1990), and (c) recommendations of state departments of education (Paisley & Hubbard, 1989).

In a recent extensive review of literature, Borders and Drury (1992) identified the developmental focus as one of four core components of effective school counseling programs. Developmental theory provides the foundation for the implementation of such programs. This theoretical approach (a) assumes that people progress through a sequence of qualitatively different stages as they interact with their environment, and (b) includes the work of a number of individuals in specific domains:

Piaget (cognitive development)
Kohlberg (ethical reasoning-justice dimension)
Gilligan (ethical reasoning-responsiveness dimension)
Selman (interpersonal understanding)
Hunt (conceptual level)
Loevinger (ego development)
Erikson (psychosocial development)
Super (career development)
Havighurst (developmental tasks)

What contribution does this array of literature provide for school counseling programs? According to Borders and Drury, the

> program content, goals, and interventions should reflect this theoretical foundation. The developmental program is proactive and preventive, helping students acquire the knowledge, skills, self-awareness, and attitudes necessary for successful mastery of normal developmental tasks. Developmental concepts are translated into specific outcomes for students; developmental principles are evident in the program plan (curriculum) and interventions. (p. 488)

Specifically, developmental theory has implications for individual counseling, small-group counseling, classroom sessions, and consultation. Examples of possible application to various program components are numerous. In individual counseling, awareness of the stage of development within a specific domain provides essential information in assessment. The developmental stage will affect the counselor's choice of strategy or approach. The focus and power of small-group work can also vary according to developmental level. Consideration of developmental stage is necessary in the selection of appropriate topics for small-group and classroom sessions, as well as in planning the sequence in which those topics are presented. Finally, sharing information about stages of development with teachers and parents can be important in promoting understanding of children and adolescents and in the related setting of appropriate expectations.

More important perhaps than specific examples of application, a developmental focus reflects a particular philosophy and commitment. The counseling program is an integral and ongoing part of the total school program, and the orientation is to primary prevention (Mosher & Sprinthall, 1971). Developmental school counseling programs are educative in nature, rather than remedial. Facilitating development requires the provision of experiences and environments that appropriately challenge and support students.

Unfortunately, however, many school counselors, although aware of the emphasis on developmental programming, are unsure of how to put it into practice. Consequently, the tendency is to rely primarily on traditional roles and crisis-intervention approaches. In response to Borders and Drury, Gerler (1992) agreed completely with the developmental focus, yet expressed significant concern over how this focus is translated into practice. Often what we know is ignored, as we offer all students the same experiences regardless of developmental differences, or as we provide support and rarely challenge. The professional literature provides us with a great deal of knowledge concerning how individuals develop psychologically and how we can facilitate that development. The time has come in school counseling programs to take advantage of what we know and begin to implement truly comprehensive developmental programs based on solid and theoretical foundations. As this focus is appropriately utilized, the need for crisis intervention and remediation is likely to be significantly reduced.

References

American School Counselor Association. (1990). *The role of the school counselor.* Alexandria, VA: Author.

Borders, L.D., & Drury, S. (1992). Comprehensive school counseling programs: A review for policy makers and practitioners. *Journal of Counseling and Development, 70*(4), 487–498.

Gerler, E. (1992). What we know about school counseling: A reaction to Borders and Drury. *Journal of Counseling and Development, 70*(4), 499–501.

Glosoff, H.L., & Kopowicz, C.L. (1990). *Children achieving potential: An introduction to elementary school counseling and state-level policies.* Alexandria, VA: American Counseling Association.

Gysbers, N., & Henderson, P. (1994). *Developing and managing your school guidance program,* (2 ed.). Alexandria, VA: American Counseling Association.

Mosher, R., & Sprinthall, N. (1971). Deliberate psychological education. *Counseling Psychologist, 2*(4), 3–82.

Myrick, R. (1987). *Developmental guidance and counseling: A practical approach.* Minneapolis, MN: Educational Media Corporation.

Paisley, P.O., & Hubbard, G.T. (1989). School counseling: State officials' perceptions of certification and employment trends. *Counselor Education and Supervision, 29*(2), 60–70.

PART ONE

DEVELOPMENTAL THEORY: CONCEPTS AND IMPACT ON SCHOOL COUNSELING PROGRAMS

CHAPTER 1

Concepts and Use of Developmental Theories

From the developmental perspective, behavior is not the result of a single cause, but of multiple causes. Human actions are explained as the result of heredity interacting with environment interacting with time. Inherited potential can be nourished or stifled depending on the type, amount, and quality of the environmental encounters, and on when those encounters occur. They can occur too early or too late to be of optimum benefit.

Children and adolescents within American schools develop in a variety of domains and at a variety of rates. To offer appropriate interventions, school personnel must be aware of the key concepts from developmental theory and practice. This chapter provides a general overview of some of the domains of development, an understanding of how development occurs, and guidelines for promoting development.

Domains of Development

Cognitive Development

Piaget (1950) provided us with a framework for understanding cognitive or intellectual development (see Table 1). Through careful ques-

TABLE 1
Piaget's Stages of Cognitive Development

Stage	Approximate Age Correlations
Sensorimotor	Birth–2 years
Intuitive or Preoperational	2–7
Concrete Operations	7–11
Formal Operations	11–18

tioning and observation of children in their natural environments, Piaget found what he considered consistent systems in thinking patterns within certain broad age ranges. These thinking patterns represented the ways children experienced and understood the world. Piaget's observations centered on the child's ability to view self as separate from the environment, and on the concepts of conservation, time, cause and effect, and number.

The consistent systems of patterns of thinking that Piaget observed were divided into four major stages of cognitive growth: (a) sensorimotor (approximate ages 0–2), (b) intuitive or preoperational (approximate ages 2–7), (c) concrete operations (approximate ages 7–11), and (d) formal operations (approximate ages 11–16; Piaget, 1950).

Learning in the sensorimotor period is based on what the infant is able to take in through the senses and manipulate with limited motor abilities. Experience is immediate, and no symbolization of this experience is possible. Visual pursuit and the beginning of object permanence are important components of growth within this stage. *Visual pursuit* can be described as the ability of an infant to track a moving object visually. *Object permanence* refers to the recognition that objects remain the same or continue to exist even when they cannot be seen.

The intuitive or preoperational stage represents movement beyond the immediate sensory environment. A child's ability to develop mental images is greatly expanded. This is particularly noticeable in the child's experimentation with symbolization through language. This period of development is closely associated with imagination and creativity. Imaginary friends and magical reasoning to explain events are common. The term *preoperational* in this stage description points to this as a period of preparation for the more complex skills of the next stage.

The movement to concrete operations represents a more complex system of thinking based on logic. Children in this stage are able to deal with presented problems factually and rationally. Although more sophisticated than the magical and sometimes illogical patterns associated with preoperational, the concrete operations stage is limited by the inability to move beyond the "literal truth," the concrete facts, "the how many?"

As these limits are removed, individuals move to Piaget's stage of formal operations. This stage represents the ability to think logically, rationally, and abstractly. There is a greater complexity, flexibility, and symbolization associated with this stage. Individuals are better able to see possibilities and translate synthesis of ideas to action. In formal operations, individuals are able to make generalizations based on experience and are able to begin seeing connections between current actions and future events.

Ethical Reasoning

Similar to Piaget's delineation of stages of cognitive growth, Kohlberg (1969) identified six qualitatively different stages of moral development. Table 2 outlines these stages. These stages represent how people think about and deal with moral questions. The six stages can be clustered into areas of (a) preconventional, (b) conventional, and (c) postconventional moral values.

The preconventional stages are designated as Stage I, relating to concern for self, and Stage II, which involves one-way concern about another person. Stage I thinking is associated with fear of punishment, particularly physical consequences. Authorities with power or strength will be obeyed. Stage II thinking is motivated much more by the desire to satisfy personal needs. This need might be characterized by the notions of "you scratch my back, I'll scratch yours" or "what's in it for me?"

With movement to the conventional cluster (Stages III and IV), relationships with others become two way. This concept of reciprocal relationships involves a belief that we are "good to each other." Stage III thinking is motivated by the desire for approval and acceptance and is dominated by the tendency to conform to group norms. The nice girl/good boy role is common in this stage. Stage IV thinking moves beyond specific peer-group acceptance to consideration of society at large. Concern centers on rules, maintaining social order, duty, and responsibility.

Kohlberg's postconventional ethical reasoning is determined by principled thought. In Stage V, there is an emphasis on societal and legal

TABLE 2
Kohlberg's Stages of Moral Growth

Basis of Judgment	Stage of Development	Characteristics of Stage
Preconventional moral values reside in external, quasi-physical happenings, in bad acts, or in quasi-physical needs rather in persons and standards	Stage 1	Obedience and punishment orientation; egocentric deference to superior power or prestige, or a trouble-avoiding set; objective responsibility
	Stage 2	Naively egoistic orientation; right action is that instrumentally satisfying one's own and occasionally other's needs; awareness that value is relative to each person's needs and perspectives; naive egalitarianism and orientation to exchange and reciprocity
Conventional moral values reside in performing good or right roles, in maintaining the conventional order, and in meeting other's expectations	Stage 3	Orientation to approval and to pleasing and helping others; conformity to stereotypical images of majority or natural role behavior, and judgment by intentions
	Stage 4	Orientation to doing one's duty and to showing respect for authority and maintaining the given social order for its own sake; regard for earned expectations of others
Postconventional moral values are derived from principles that can be applied universally	Stage 5	Contractual-legalistic orientation; recognition of an arbitrary element in rules of expectations for the sake of agreement; duty defined in terms of contract, general avoidance of violations of the will or rights of others, or of the majority will and welfare
	Stage 6	Orientation to conscience or principles, not only to ordained social rules but to principles of choice appealing to logical universality and consistency; conscience is a directing agent, together with mutual respect and trust

Note. From *Adolescent Psychology: A Developmental View* (p. 188) by N.A. Sprinthall and W.A. Collins, 1988, New York: McGraw-Hill. Copyright 1985 by McGraw-Hill. Reprinted by permission.

contracts without legal absolutes. Change can be determined by consensus, with a motivating concern being "the greatest good for the greatest number." Stage VI represents a system of thinking through moral questions based on universal ethical principles that would be applicable to everyone. This stage of thinking would reflect justice as a categorical imperative: acting as one would want all others to act. Such a just society could be created by a rational group of individuals who designed the rules for the culture (including the roles, expectations, and rewards) knowing they would have to live there, but not knowing what role they would play.

Gilligan (1982) added to our understanding of ethical reasoning by addressing the "different voice" heard in processing moral dilemmas. In research with women, in addition to the justice dimension identified by Kohlberg, Gilligan described a responsiveness or care dimension. This different voice focuses on consideration given to the effects of decisions on self and others.

Conceptual Level

David Hunt has centered his work on differences in conceptual levels particularly as they relate to education. Conceptual level as a developmental domain includes both cognitive and interpersonal dimensions. Hunt (1978) noted that the general definition of *conceptual level* is "in terms of (1) increasing conceptual complexity as indicated by discrimination, differentiation, and integration and (2) increasing interpersonal maturity as indicated by self-definition and self-other relations" (p. 2). Conceptual level also seems to follow a stage sequence in its development.

The lowest stage (0) reflects an impulsive, negative, and unsocialized view of the world. This stage is exclusively centered on concern for self. Stage 1 is generally characterized as concrete and stereotyped. Motivation is on that which is socially acceptable or is in deference to authority. Issues are seen dichotomously—right or wrong, good or bad.

Stage 2 conceptual level reflects an openness to others' ideas, some evaluation of alternatives, some tolerance of ambiguity and uncertainty, and an increased awareness of emotions. This stage is also moving toward innerdirectedness. Stage 3 conceptual level is characterized by the consideration given to weighing alternatives, the concern for one's own ideas as well as others, the consideration given to the consequences of actions, compromise and synthesis in problem solving, and, finally, an acceptance of responsibility for the course of action chosen.

Sprinthall and Sprinthall (1981) characterized three of these stages as follows:

> Stage 1—Low Conceptual Level. Generally, thinking is concrete and stereotyped. There is a single "right" way to learn. Rules are fixed and unchangeable. Obedience to authority is unquestioned. Problem-solving tends to be rigid. Social desirability and pleasing others are strong. Individuals at stage one are anxious for closure and tend to seek highly structured learning activities.
> Stage 2—Moderate Conceptual Level. There is some evidence and tolerance for uncertainty and ambiguity and a developing awareness of alternatives. Individuals at stage two have openness to new ideas and an increased independence in thinking (inner-directedness). There is an increased awareness of emotions and use of inductive inquiry.
> Stage 3—High Conceptual Level. There is evidence of integration and synthesis both in complex intellectual and interpersonal areas. Individuals at stage three are able to weigh and balance alternatives, simultaneously processing their own views and those of others. Closure is temporary and these individuals are able to employ successive approximation. Principles are used in decision-making and full responsiblity is accepted for the consequences of behavior. (pp. 376–377)

Psychosocial Development

Erikson (1963) outlined eight stages of psychosocial development. Each of these stages is characterized by a particular developmental crisis. These crises are sometimes seen as conflicts, struggles, or choices. Erikson's stages represent a life-span theory focused on healthy development. Table 3 provides an overview of these crises.

Erikson's bipolar crises are: (a) basic trust versus mistrust (0–18 months), (b) autonomy versus shame (18 months–3 years), (c) initiative versus guilt (3–6), (d) mastery versus inferiority (7–12), (e) identity versus diffusion (12–18), (f) intimacy versus isolation (18–30), (g) generativity versus stagnation (30–60), and (h) integrity versus despair (60–). Initiative versus guilt, mastery versus inferiority, identity versus diffusion, and intimacy versus isolation are the most relevant crises for school-age children and adolescents. When early childhood experiences have not allowed the positive resolution of earlier crises, the issues associated with trust versus mistrust and autonomy versus shame will also have to be revisited.

As children attempt to resolve the crisis of initiative versus guilt, they are discovering what kind of persons they are, particularly as that relates to gender. Although this crisis is loosely associated with an

TABLE 3
Erikson's Crises for Psychosocial Growth

Age	Crises
Birth to 18 months	Basic trust versus mistrust
18 months–3 years	Autonomy versus shame
3–6 years	Initiative versus guilt
7–12 years	Mastery versus inferiority
12–18 years	Identity versus diffusion
18–30 years	Intimacy versus isolation
30–60 years	Generativity versus stagnation
60–	Integrity versus despair

age range of 3–6 years old, school-age children are often still dealing with finding their places as males or females. Children seek and copy appropriate adult role models whether at home or school. This is a time period in which children need to be supported in their hope that they will grow up to be real adults. Ridicule by adults rather than reassurance can result in a more negative resolution of the crisis, with an emphasis on guilt.

As children enter school, the next Eriksonian crisis, mastery versus inferiority, becomes apparent. Children are exposed to many new activities and experiences as they begin school. There are numerous opportunities to learn new skills and "ways of being" both in the classroom and on the playing field. Children want to learn at this stage and are intensely curious. Learning at this stage is best handled as an active process, harnessing the interest and energy that children already have. Positively resolving this crisis will have long-lasting effects on the individual's self-concept and sense of self-efficacy.

The crisis of personal identity associated with adolescence is the most widely researched of Erikson's ideas. This definition of self is critical in moving toward adulthood. Positive resolution of this crisis involves integrating perceptions of self with the way others see us. This crisis occurs as individuals are caught between two worlds—childhood and adulthood. They are too old for some things and not old enough for others. Adolescents are in constant transition and are dealing with physical changes, emotional turmoil, and new social arenas simultaneously. Adults within adolescents' lives can offer essential support and guidance toward personal growth by providing increasing amounts of independence and responsibility.

The final crisis of interest with school-age children is intimacy versus isolation. This crisis involves the ability to build healthy and successful relationships and connections with others. Although this crisis was originally seen as one encountered after self-definition, later speculations have proposed that determining our own identity is in part carried out through our attempts at relationships with others. However, most research still supports that true intimacy cannot be achieved without a sense of personal identity. Perhaps the key to these findings can be explained through the definition used for intimacy. *Intimacy* is described as "the ability for mutual psychological as well as physical relationships with another person" (Sprinthall & Collins, 1988, p. 170). This mutuality requires that individuals be able to consider both their own and the other person's thoughts, feelings, and needs. This process is not limited to sexual intimacy, but also includes close friendships. Without successful resolution of this crisis, individuals tend to be isolated by their own self-absorption.

Interpersonal Development

Selman (1980) outlined levels of interpersonal understanding based on reasoning related to social judgment and social decision making. Of particular significance in Selman's work is the concept of *perspective taking*. This social task refers to the ability to infer or understand another's position or perspective. Selman identified five levels of interpersonal understanding related to perspective taking: (0) egocentric, (1) subjective, (2) self-reflective, (3) mutual, and (4) in-depth and societal-symbolic. These levels of interpersonal understanding reflect beliefs about both other people and relationships. Without the ability to understand one's self as separate from others and the relationship as an interactive process, children and adolescents are limited in the interactions that they may have. Table 4 describes Selman's levels of interpersonal understanding.

Career Development

A number of theorists (Ginzberg, Ginzburg, Axelrad, & Herma, 1951; Super, 1972; Tiedeman & O'Hara, 1963) have approached career choice from a developmental perspective. Ginzberg et al. identified stages related to occupational choice entitled fantasy, tentative, and realistic. Tiedeman and O'Hara tied career development to Erikson's ego-relevant crises, noting that as the ego develops, career-relevant decision-making possibilities also develop (Zunker, 1990). Super's approach is generally considered the most comprehensive and cen-

CONCEPTS AND USE OF DEVELOPMENTAL THEORIES

TABLE 4
Selman's Levels of Interpersonal Understanding

Level	Concept of Persons	Concept of Relations
0: Egocentric perspective taking (under 6 years)	Undifferentiated: confuses internal (feelings, intentions) with external (appearance, actions) characteristics of others	Egocentric: fails to recognize that self and others have different feelings and thoughts as well as external physical characteristics
1: Subjective perspective taking (ages 5–9)	Differentiated: distinguishes feelings and intentions from actions and appearances	Subjective: recognizes that others may feel and think differently than self—that everyone is subjective but has limited conceptions of how these different persons may affect each other (e.g., gifts make people happy, regardless of how appropriate they are)
2: Self-reflective or reciprocal perspective taking (ages 7–12)	Second-person: can reflect on own thoughts and realizes that others can do as well; realizes appearances may be deceptive about true feelings	Reciprocal: puts self in others' shoes and realizes others may do same; these thoughts and feelings, not merely actions, become basis for interaction; however, the two subjective perspectives are not assumed to be influencing each other
3. Mutual perspective taking (ages 10–15)	Third-person: knows that self and others act and reflect on effects of their actions on themselves; recognizes own immediate subjective perspective and also realizes that it fits into own more general attitudes and values	Mutual: can imagine another persons' perspective on oneself and one's actions, coordinates other's inferred view with own view (i.e., sees self as others see one); thus come to view relationships as ongoing mutual sharing of social satisfactions or understanding
4. In-depth and societal-symbolic perspective taking (ages 12–adult)	In-depth: recognizes that persons are unique, complex combinations of their own histories; furthermore, realizes that persons may not always understand their own motivations (i.e., that there may be unconscious psychological processes)	Societal-symbolic: individuals may form perspectives on each other at different levels, from common values or appreciation of very abstract moral, legal, or social notions

Note. From *Adolescent Psychology: A Developmental View* (p. 120) by N. A. Sprinthall and W. A. Collins, 1988, New York: McGraw-Hill. Copyright 1988 by McGraw-Hill. Reprinted by permission.

TABLE 5
Ginzberg's Periods of Career Development

Period	Description
Fantasy (childhood)	Playful orientation to activities; gradually play becomes more work oriented
Tentative (early adolescence)	Transition stage focused on identification of interests, abilities, work rewards, values
Realistic (middle adolescence)	Integration of abilities and interests; substages of exploration, crystallization, specification

Note. Adapted from *Career Counseling: Applied Concepts of Life Planning* (p. 23) by V. Zunker, 1990, Pacific Grove, CA: Brooks/Cole. Copyright 1990 by Brooks/Cole.

ters on the implementation of self-concept while identifying developmental stages, tasks, and patterns. Super additionally considered the concept of career maturity, indicating the readiness of individuals to participate in or benefit from various career-related activities. Developmental frameworks have been particularly helpful in designing career education sequences. Tables 5 and 6 provide an overview of vocational developmental stages outlined by Ginzberg and Super.

TABLE 6
Super's Stages of Vocational Development

Stage	Description
Growth (birth–middle adolescence)	development of capacity, attitudes, interests, needs associated with self-concept
Exploratory (middle–late adolescence)	tentative phase; choices are narrowed but not finalized
Establishment (midlife)	trial and stabilization in work environments
Maintenance (midlife–65)	adjustment process to improve working position and situation
Decline (65+)	movement toward retirement

Note. Adapted from *Career Counseling: Applied Concepts of Life Planning* (pp. 25–26) by V. Zunker, 1991, Pacific Grove, CA: Brooks/Cole. Copyright 1991 by Brooks/Cole.

Developmental Tasks

Although not truly representing a developmental domain, Havighurst (1972) designated certain tasks that emerge at certain ages or stages of development. Havighurst defined *developmental tasks* as sets of specific challenges ". . . which arise at or about a certain period in the life of an individual, successful achievement of which leads to . . . happiness and to success with later tasks, while failure leads to unhappiness in the individual, disapproval by the society and difficulty with later tasks" (p. 2). Havighurst acknowledged the influence of biology, psychology, and culture on the experience of these tasks. Table 7 out-

TABLE 7
Havighurst's Developmental Tasks

Stage	Tasks
Early Childhood	(1) Learning to form simple concepts of social and physical reality (2) Learning to distinguish right and wrong and developing a conscience (3) Learning to talk (4) Learning to differentiate by gender
Middle Childhood	(1) Developing concepts for everyday living including basic physical and academic skills (2) Developing conscience, morality, and a scale of values (3) Achieving personal independence (4) Learning to get along with agemates (5) Learning an appropriate masculine or feminine social role
Adolescence	(1) Accepting one's physique and using the body effectively (2) Achieving a masculine or feminine social role (3) Achieving new and more mature relations with agemates of both sexes (4) Achieving emotional independence of parents and other adults (5) Preparing for an economic career (6) Preparing for marriage and family life (7) Desiring and achieving socially responsible behavior (8) Acquiring a set of values and an ethical system as a guide to behavior (9) Achieving physical maturity

Note. Adapted from *Child and Adolescent Development* by M. J. Gander and H. W. Gardiner, 1981, Boston: Little, Brown. Copyright 1981 by Little, Brown.

lines the tasks that Havighurst associated with school-age children and adolescents.

How Development Occurs

Mechanisms of Change

Across these domains, changes in the cognitive structures are possible through interaction with the environment. As individuals encounter something slightly different in the environment, a process for understanding or adapting the new to the old is set in motion. Piaget (1950) identified this process of adaptation as one composed of two complementary parts: assimilation and accommodation. Assimilation refers to the attempt to make the new fit what is already known. The parts of the new object, situation, or experience that do not quite fit require the process of accommodation or a modification of our organizational system. The internal structure must be changed. This change in the existing organization will in turn result in a more complex structure for understanding and thinking. Piaget called this process of restoring balance *equilibration*, a central feature to developmental growth. Additional facilitators of change that have an impact on this process are the maturation process, specific experiences with the environment, and social interactions. Because encountering "the new" (either concretely or abstractly) is necessary for cognitive growth, these facilitators provide the necessary new objects, situations, or dilemmas.

Developmental Assumptions

Within developmental psychology, there are also certain underlying assumptions that are of central significance and that merit restatement (Sprinthall & Collins, 1988):

- Human beings have a strong urge to derive meaning from experience. R.W. White (1959) designates this as competence motivation, an inborn need to grow and develop mastery of the environment.
- Human beings have a system or style or method to process information from the environment. This system is called a stage and represents a distinctive, unique, and consistent cognitive ensemble.

- These stages are qualitatively different from each other. Therefore growth represents qualitative transformations rather than quantitative. A child is not a miniature adult.
- Stages are in a sequence organized according to level of complexity. Growth occurs in sequence through the hierarchy from less to more complex. An individual rarely goes back to a previous stage. An adult acting childlike is qualitatively different from a child simply being a child.
- Growth through the stages is not automatic. Appropriate interaction between the individual and the environment is required.
- There is a consistent relationship between stage and behavior. Stage gives a reasonably good indication of behavior.
- Stage growth occurs in a variety of domains or aspects of being human. This growth may be uneven. It is in fact unlikely that an individual would function at the highest stages of development in all possible domains.(pp. 22–23)

Promoting Development

Components of Successful Programs

In examining programs that have been successful in promoting development, certain components have emerged as significant. These components have been identified as role taking, reflection, balance, challenge, support, and continuity (Sprinthall & Thies-Sprinthall, 1983).

Role taking refers to the placement of an individual in a new situation or experential set that requires "stretching" or the use of slightly more complex skills and processing than currently employed. The role taking needs to be real and significant, rather than simulated or routine. This experience also needs to be examined through *reflection*, with individuals being given an opportunity to process feelings and to understand their experiences from different perspectives.

Balance is also apparently needed in relation to challenge and support. As outlined earlier, Piaget's state of disequilibrium is central to development. Although this state of dissonance may be necessary and growth producing, it is not without pain. Personal support for individuals facing *challenge* is essential.

Finally, programs designed to promote development need to provide *continuity*. This component involves a somewhat longer time commit-

TABLE 8
Dilemma Examples

Dilemma	Description
Dilemma 1: Heinz's Problem	In Europe a woman was near death from a special kind of cancer. There was one drug that the doctors thought might save her. It was a form of radium that a druggist in the same town had recently discovered. The drug was expensive to make, but the druggist was charging 10 times what the drug cost him to make. He paid $200 for the radium and charged $2000 for a small dose of the drug. The sick woman's husband, Heinz, went to everyone he knew to borrow the money, but he could only get together about $1000, which is half of what it cost. He told the druggist that his wife was dying, and asked him to sell it cheaper or let him pay later. But the druggist said, "No, I discovered the drug and I'm going to make money from it." So Heinz got desperate and broke into the man's store to steal the drug for his wife. 1. Should Heinz have done that? 2. Was it actually wrong or right? Why?
Dilemma 2: Alex's Problem	Joe's father promised he could go to camp if he earned the $50 for it, and then changed his mind and asked Joe to give him the money he had earned. Joe lied and said he had only earned $10 and went to camp using the other $40 he had made. Before he went, he told his younger brother Alex about the money and about lying to their father. Should Alex tell their father? 1. What are the reasons to tell? 2. To not tell?

Note. From *Adolescent Psychology: A Developmental View* (p. 189) by N. A. Sprinthall and W. A. Collins, 1988, New York: McGraw-Hill. Copyright 1988 by McGraw-Hill. Reprinted by permission.

ment—most probably 6 months to 1 year to be effective. Brief interventions may be appropriate for sharing information or general awareness, but not for promoting development.

Dilemma Discussions

In schools, a particular approach used to promote development is dilemma discussion (Sprinthall & Sprinthall, 1981). This involves the presentation of open-ended dilemmas for discussion and analysis. The teacher or counselor serves as a facilitator. The purpose of discussion is for students to think through and articulate their own reasoning about decisions. The process also gives them an opportunity to hear the reasoning and ideas of others. Facilitators are not involved in lecturing or providing "right answers," but instead focus on clarifying the levels of reasoning.

A variety of types of dilemmas are possible. Those used by Kohlberg in his research can be presented, such as Heinz and the drug to save his wife's life (see Table 8). Others more closely associated with student experience might be written based on choices concerning cheating, drugs, or sexual activity. Students familiar with the dilemma process can also be encouraged to construct their own situations for discussion. Additionally, many dilemmas emerge within existing curricula in social studies and literature. Taking advantage of these for discussion as they arise is an excellent method of integrating the promotion of development within the current school program.

Plus-One Reasoning

A factor of considerable significance in dilemma discussion is plus-one reasoning. Within developmental domains, individuals have a modal stage of development, indicating their general method of processing experience. Although students will be able to understand all of the levels of reasoning below their own, they will only comprehend one stage above. The slightly more complex reasoning of one stage above is generally attractive or intriguing to individuals. More than that is overwhelming and will not be beneficial in any real way. Allowing students to listen to reasoning one level up from their own tends to provoke thought and in turn promote development.

Significant Role-Taking Experiences

Providing students with opportunities to take on meaningful new roles can also be a significant piece in promoting development. Peer-tutoring and peer-helping programs have been very successful in providing these types of opportunities. These programs are often beneficial to both parties. Service projects in which students volunteer time within the community can also offer new challenges. These projects might involve working in a nursing home, serving as a candystriper at a local hospital, or assisting with after-school activities for younger children through a recreational department. Whether serving as a peer helper or a community volunteer, it is important for students to process and reflect on these experiences in some way. Small-group sharing or personal journal writing can provide for such reflection.

Person–Environment Fit

More important, perhaps, than any single strategy or approach is the concept of person-to-environment fit. To facilitate development, teachers and counselors need to match and then constructively mismatch the learning activities with the developmental level of the student (Hunt, 1975). This technique involves assessing where the student is, using this information or level as a starting point, and then gradually employing more complex methods of instruction. This movement toward constructive mismatch is similar to plus-one reasoning, with an underlying purpose of provoking thought and promoting development to the next stage.

Hunt emphasized the importance of this developmental view in relation to creating appropriate environments:

> Maintaining a developmental perspective becomes very important in implementing person-environment matching because a teacher should not only take account of a student's contemporaneous needs by providing whatever structure he presently requires, but also view his present need for structure on a developmental continuum along which growth toward independence and less need for structure is the long-term objective. (p. 221)

This message is important for counselors to internalize also. We need to: (a) provide the optimal levels of structure and experience for students' current levels of functioning, and (b) design a sufficiently challenging environment in which they can move along that developmental continuum. The outcomes associated with such movement would be more complex structures for processing experience and higher levels of cognitive, ethical, and interpersonal maturity. It is unlikely that counselors can create these environments alone. Instead, teachers, counselors, and administrators need to collaborate to provide the type of educational experiences most likely to facilitate development.

Summary

Developmental theory provides an excellent framework for designing, developing, and implementing school counseling programs. Counselors can use information from a variety of domains to gain a clearer understanding of where students are and how their development might be encouraged. Specifically, developmental theory has implications for individual counseling, group work, and consultation. Using this perspective, the counseling program does not exist in isolation, but is an integral and ongoing part of the total school program focused on primary prevention.

CHAPTER 2

The Impact of Developmental Theory on Individual Counseling

One component of the school counselor's role that is consistently recognized in the literature is individual counseling. In the implementation of developmental school counseling programs, the question then arises of how to use what we know from developmental theory in individual interventions. There are, in fact, several implications. Although the importance of the relationship is central regardless of age or stage, the choice of specific approach or strategy will vary based on developmental level. This chapter reviews relationship building, outlines examples of the questions and issues to consider in developmental assessment, and suggests a variety of potential strategies.

Relationship Building

Regardless of theoretical approach, the *relationship* between counselor and child or adolescent is central to the helping process. The work of Rogers (1942) and Carkhuff (1972) provided information and insight on exactly how significant the relationship is. The characteristics of a true helping relationship, and the corresponding stages of helping identified in client-centered approaches, continue to be important for counselors to keep in mind as they make connections with young people. Gordon's (1974) work in effective communication also provides helpful information concerning some of the roadblocks to avoid in building healthy relationships.

Characteristics of a Helping Relationship

In facilitating the development of the relationship, the qualities of *respect*, *empathy*, and *unconditional positive regard* have been identified as necessary components. For children and adolescents, these are as important as they are with adults. Often children are viewed as somehow "less than real people," rather than truly appreciated for their own uniqueness. When adults can convey their acceptance in a genuine way, they have given children and adolescents a special gift. This *genuineness* is critical in building a positive relationship, and it is important to remember that young people have very sensitive "radar" in recognizing phoniness. Unfortunately, there are too many individuals working with children who are not able to truly enjoy or respect them. This makes those who are really "there" for young people particularly special. For counselors and other adults working with children and adolescents, the importance of the time spent in building relationships, really getting to know the individual, and understanding the world from their perspective should never be minimized.

In moving the helping relationship toward action orientations, the components of *concreteness*, *confrontation*, and *immediacy* become important. Young people need adults in their lives who can lovingly challenge them concerning their thoughts, feelings, and behaviors. They sometimes (as do adults) need to be confronted with discrepancies between their words and their deeds. This confrontation needs to be done in concrete and specific terms, not vague generalities. This *specificity* is another critical component in being helpful. To say "I don't like what you did" is not particularly helpful. To be able to point to a particular action and to offer alternative behaviors is much more appropriate.

Stages of a Helping Relationship

Relationship building does not spontaneously occur. Instead, it takes patience and work. Particularly in counseling with young people, the temptation exists to provide "the quick fix," to tell a child what to do to make life better. We need to remind ourselves to slow down and use the stages of helping. First, allow individuals to explore the problem thoroughly. Give students time to say what they need to say. Through the use of reflection and feedback, clarify the central concern. Make sure the child or adolescent agrees with you about what that concern is. Only then does movement toward action make sense. Brainstorming alternatives, considering consequences, and committing to a plan of action are possible only after you are sure you know what the problem is. Although you do not need for a child to give you a great deal of tangential information, you also do not need to rush headlong toward action either. Allow yourself the time to build the relationship and understand the world (and the problem) from the young person's perspective.

Roadblocks to Effective Communication

In building any type of relationship, effective communication is necessary. Our responses to others can open the door to continuing interaction or slam it shut. Gordon's work gives us helpful information concerning obstacles to effective communication. He identified responses that can dismiss feelings, show a lack of confidence in students' abilities to solve their own problems, impose guilt, ridicule, or in some other way minimize and belittle the student as a unique person. These roadblocks to be avoided are outlined in Table 9. More appropriate methods of responding involve passive and active listening, acknowledgments, and invitations to continue to talk. These strategies are

TABLE 9
Roadblocks to Effective Communication

1. Ordering, commanding, directing
2. Warning, threatening
3. Moralizing, preaching, giving "shoulds" and "oughts"
4. Advising, offering solutions or suggestions
5. Teaching, lecturing, giving logical arguments
6. Judging, criticizing, disagreeing, blaming
7. Name-calling, stereotyping, labeling
8. Interpreting, analyzing, diagnosing
9. Praising, agreeing, giving positive evaluations
10. Reassuring, sympathizing, consoling, supporting
11. Questioning, probing, interrogating, cross-examining
12. Withdrawing, distracting, being sarcastic, humoring, diverting

Note. Adapted from *T.E.T.: Teacher Effectiveness Training* by T. Gordon, 1974, New York: Dave McKay. Copyright 1974 by David McKay.

particularly important in the initial stages of helping (exploring and clarifying).

Avoiding these roadblocks and practicing principles of effective communication can enhance relationships. Counselors can become more effective in making connections to the young person's world and empowering the child or adolescent. An individual is much more likely to share his or her world with someone who has really listened and who has valued the experiences, feelings, and perspectives presented.

Assessment

As counselors gather information about exactly what the situation is, assessment concerning developmental level is equally important. Using developmental theory as a backdrop, there are numerous questions to be asked. Cognitively, is this student capable of abstract thought? Ethically, what motivates this student's behavior? Interpersonally, is the student able to take another's perspective or understand a problem or situation from another person's point of view? Conceptually, how much structure does this student need within the counseling process? Which of Erikson's crises is the student most clearly attempting to resolve? Which of Havighurst's tasks is the student attempting to master? Answering these questions can have significant implications for how a counselor might proceed in individual counseling.

Cognitively, if the student has not yet progressed to abstract thought, then a number of counseling interventions that require generalization or the ability to make future prediction based on present circumstances would be inappropriate. The student would be dealing with situations too concretely in the "here and now" to be able to benefit from those interventions.

Understanding where a student is cognitively can also be helpful in recognizing what is appropriate at particular ages and stages. A 6-year-old at the intuitive or preoperational stage of cognitive development with an imaginary friend is quite normal; a 14-year-old carrying on the same relationship would suggest a need for intervention. Concrete thinkers stubbornly holding onto a problem-solving strategy or perception based on "the *most* facts" is probably to be expected. Even with the movement to formal operations, the adolescent's egocentrism needs to be taken into account in the counseling process. In an adult, the preoccupation with one's own uniqueness and the corresponding obsession with being the focus of everyone's attention might be diagnosed as narcissism or paranoia, whereas in an adolescent these are actually quite normal. The certainty that their own experiences are unique to the human process is referred to as the *personal fable*, and the notion that everyone's attention is focused on them as the *imaginary audience*. Most individuals who have survived adolescence can relate to both sets of feelings.

Ethically, if the student's behavior is motivated by a desire to please others, then counselors must be particularly sensitive to tendencies to agree to observations or plans of action simply to please the adult. Although this desire to please may help in motivating more appropriate or effective ways of behaving, the counselor needs to be aware of what is occurring, rather than confuse it with an internal motivation. This tendency can be frustrating within the counseling process when students say what we want to hear concerning a plan of action and then never follow through. Knowing that they are trying to please us does not make the problem go away, but does give us insight into why this behavior is occurring and grounds for challenging the student.

Interpersonally, the ability to take another's point of view also has significance in individual counseling. Many problems that are presented by young people involve relationship issues. Attempting to deal with those if the child is incapable of understanding another person's point of view (or that the other person even has a point of view that is different from his or her own) can be challenging. We sometimes assume that children have this capacity and proceed with counseling as if they do. If they are interested in pleasing us, they will say what we want to hear, nod and smile at appropriate moments, perhaps without a clue about what we are suggesting. Sometimes a strategy as simple as adapting a role play may provide the necessary insight. For some children, requiring them to physically change places can assist them in trying to "be" another person. For students capable of abstract thought, this physical exchange might not be necessary. Instead, they would be able to make that generalization or observation on their own and draw their own conclusions. Providing young people with opportunities to hear others' perspectives and views can be a valuable way of promoting development within the interpersonal domain.

As an additional example, consider the student at a lower level of conceptual development as identified by Hunt. That student would need much more structure within the counseling process. The counselor would be well served to be very specific with the student concerning the goals and process for counseling. Homework assignments and guided practice for interactions would be particularly helpful. Careful monitoring and follow-up would also be desirable. With a student at a higher level of conceptual development, there would be more of a need for independence, more tolerance for ambiguity, and less need for highly structured counseling experiences. The counselor would not need to be as concrete in presentation or provide as much practice for the student in carrying out action plans. In fact, the student might be resistant to such detail.

Finally, identifying the specific crisis or task that the student is attempting to resolve can also be helpful. The adults in children's lives can assist by providing the necessary experiences to promote growth. Provision of appropriate adult role models, activities to learn new skills, or opportunities for new responsibilities could all be appropriate interventions, depending on the particular crisis or task. Sometimes interventions to promote trust and encourage autonomy will also be necessary based on the lack of positive resolution of these crises during early childhood.

Strategies

Other than the particular nature of the problem, the age and stage of the student with whom a counselor is working will most clearly influence the strategies selected for use in interventions. Approaches that might be appropriate in working with an adult simply are not helpful in reaching a 5-year-old child. As indicated in the previous section, an adolescent capable of abstract thought would be dealt with very differently from a young person who was reasoning very concretely. Reliance on a single approach or set of strategies would severely limit what a counselor could offer to the wide range of developmental levels represented by students in kindergarten through 12th grade. This section attempts to remind the reader, through examples, of the variety of specific strategies available.

Play Media and Expressive Arts

Very often children do not have the experience or vocabulary to conceptualize or express their concerns and issues verbally. Instead, they are much better at working through their issues through the use of play media and expressive arts. Play is their work, and the selected medium becomes their language. Even with older adolescents, sometimes expressive arts provide the method of accessing issues and experiences that cognitive approaches cannot reach. Adolescents may have learned to defend themselves cognitively from painful events that they wish to forget. The "blockage" may reflect an earlier stage of development in which some crisis was not resolved.

The types of media that can be creatively used in counseling are limited only by the imagination. Paints, crayons, toys, clay, sand, and water can be used by children and adolescents to create scenes, events, and individuals. Music, drama, and journal writing can provide outlets for self-expression. The use of quality children's literature can provoke thought and discussion, offer opportunities to see others' perspectives, and, in general, promote development.

Various theoretical perspectives provide frameworks for conducting counseling sessions using play media. Resources are available from child-centered (Axline, 1947, 1964; Landreth, 1991), Gestalt (Oaklander, 1977), Adlerian (Kottman & Warlick, 1989), and Jungian (Allen, 1988) approaches. The approaches vary in the amount of external structure given to the student and in the amount of interpretation given within the process. All share the recognition of the developmental appropriateness of play as a counseling intervention with many children and some adolescents.

Gestalt Approaches

In addition to those strategies associated with the use of expressive arts, Gestalt therapy offers several interventions that are helpful in working with students at various developmental stages. Three particular examples of these strategies are *topdog/underdog*, *empty chair*, and *fantasy games*.

Topdog is the "you should" voice in our lives; underdog, the "I want." Using two chairs and moving back and forth, the student can conduct his or her own debate. This activity could be adapted for older adolescents by allowing them to make "should" and "want" lists. After the student has exhausted all arguments on either side, the counselor can process the activity. With hope, the process will allow the student to integrate the shoulds and wants to make an effective choice. This activity helps children and adolescents begin to see the bipolarities in everyday life.

The empty chair strategy is perhaps one of the most widely used specific strategies from Gestalt therapy. This technique can be used to resolve conflict or to handle unresolved anger, fear, or frustration. The child or adolescent would sit in one chair and say to the empty chair whatever he or she needed or wanted to say. Moving to the other chair, the student would project a response. This strategy can allow the student to process and explore issues and can give the counselor insight into the individual's perspective. Sometimes young children can participate in this activity more fully if a hypothetical person is introduced with similar concerns (Thompson & Poppen, 1992: cited in Thompson & Rudolph, 1992). Similar to the advantages of using puppets in play, children can sometimes explore the problems of an imaginary person better than they can examine their own issues.

Many fantasy games provide opportunities to explore feelings and have fun within the counseling process. With children, pretending to be an animal or special toy allows them to act out stories and describe feelings. More in-depth fantasies such as the rosebush or the wise person usually work well with all but the truly cynical or concrete. With concrete thinkers who believe fantasy is silly, sometimes it is enough to say, "I know you think this is strange, but just try it anyway." For some individuals, this "gives them permission" to be more childlike because you are making them do it. (For some, these approaches will never work. Cognitive strategies will provide better results. Watch for assumptions, however. Often the most resistant individuals may actually need these approaches to access feelings.)

Systematic Problem Solving

With concrete thinkers, or with students needing structure as part of the counseling process, systematic problem solving offers a workable approach. A number of models are available, most of which involve a step-by-step process for working through difficult situations. This process requires the student and counselor to identify the problem clearly and to project the desired outcome; to consider any strategies that have already been tried; to brainstorm alternative strategies; to review possible consequences; to make a plan of action; and to follow up as a way of monitoring outcomes. (This approach can also be helpful with abstract thinkers who have trouble committing to action in the face of all the possibilities they can see.)

Behavioral Contracts

When change in a particular behavior is the desired outcome, contracts can be a very helpful strategy. There are many similarities between the initial steps in contingency contracting and systematic problem solving. Both require clear identification of the problem, the desired outcome, and the various possible methods of solving the problem. However, with a contingency contract, additional emphases are placed on gathering baseline data and determining the consequences, either positive or negative reinforcement, which will be used if the contract is not fulfilled. Such contracts are particularly helpful for students needing a great deal of structure and for those whose ethical reasoning is motivated by physical consequences. (Sometimes, in considering the levels of ethical reasoning, we think of physical consequences in controversial forms such as paddling. Physical consequences, however, can also include time-out areas, reward systems, or restrictions of desired privileges.) The clarity and specificity of contracts are very helpful to many students in earlier stages of development.

For students at higher levels of development, some forms of behavioral contracts are still appropriate. However, a significant difference would be in the level of involvement of the counselor. With these students, the focus would be on self-management. Whereas with a younger student, the counselor would collect the baseline data, formulate the structure (with student agreement), and monitor the outcomes, students at higher stages of development would have those responsibilities themselves. These self-management approaches can provide a helpful bridge between childhood and adulthood as adolescents begin to strive for independence and attempt to determine their own identities.

Cognitive–Behavioral Approaches

Cognitive–behavioral strategies also provide useful transitions that combine a focus on specific behaviors with thought-restructuring methods. These approaches attempt to produce both behavior and feeling change. Positive (or more rational) self-talk is encouraged to accompany changes in particular behaviors. Homework assignments and identification of irrational thoughts are key components to models based on cognitive–behavioral therapy.

In working with young children using these approaches, some adaptations would need to be considered. As with any approach, the vocabulary would have to be adjusted. Although Ellis (1962) spoke of rational and irrational thoughts, Anderson (1987), in her third-grade curriculum, talked about "sparkle and mud minds" to which children can relate. Adolescents at higher stages of development will be able to talk through some of these ideas and issues. Younger children may need the concrete experience of writing down examples of negative self-talk and methods of challenging those notions. Many specific strategies would need to be adjusted also. Although relaxation training, deep-breathing activities, and reframing exercises might be appropriate at some ages and stages, the explanation and content would need to be adapted.

Several examples are available in the literature of adaptations of rational self-analysis to fit the developmental level of the child. Some suggest levels of treatment along a developmental continuum. Thompson and Rudolph (1992) cited a model developed by Winnett, Bornstein, Cogswell, and Paris (1987) for the treatment of depression in children, which

> consists of four levels of treatment: (1) behavioral procedures, such as contingent reinforcement, shaping, prompting, and modeling, to increase social interaction; (2) CBT [cognitive-behavioral therapy] interventions, which include pairing successful task completion with positive self-statements; (3) cognitive interventions, which are used with social skills training, role-playing, and self-management; and (4) self-control procedures, such as self-evaluation and self-reinforcement. (p. 143)

This model directly responds to the need for structure at lower levels of development and the corresponding movement toward increasing independence at higher stages.

Summary

Developmental theory has several implications for individual counseling. Informally assessing levels of development in various domains can provide valuable information for the counselor in selecting an appropriate strategy or approach. Using knowledge concerning where the child or adolescent is developmentally, counselors can adapt strategies from the wealth of counseling interventions.

CHAPTER 3

The Impact of Developmental Theory on Group Counseling

The school counselor's role is not limited to individual counseling. In fact, in a comprehensive and developmental school counseling program, individual counseling rarely represents more than one half of the use of the counselor's time. School counselors often provide services, information, and developmental programs in either large or small groups. The use of groups as a vehicle for delivery of services is appropriate for several reasons. Comprehensive and developmental programs imply accessibility for all students. With the high student-to-counselor ratios present in most situations, reliance on individual interventions is not feasible.

Beyond this logistical issue, some concerns are much more appropriately and productively addressed in groups. Working individually with students who have poor social skills or difficulty resolving conflicts with others may not be the best intervention. Instead, group situations that allow them to practice new skills and behaviors may be more effective. Students can confront each other in groups in acceptable ways with the guidance provided by a facilitator. Students can also support each other in groups. Often young people believe that they are the only ones who feel a particular way. There is a major difference between an adult saying "you're not the only one" and a peer really showing them they are not alone.

An additional rationale for group work can be found in what we know about how development occurs. One method of promoting development involves the challenge of hearing other perspectives, particularly those one level up from our own. Groups provide such an opportunity to discuss different approaches or views concerning the same problem or issue. Groups also represent a more authentic approximation of the actual environments in which children and adolescents live. Although there are certainly problems that must be dealt with on an individual basis, there is also a therapeutic advantage to dealing with concerns in the context within which they occur. In group work, we are not only affecting individual change, but also providing for adjustments in the environment.

In practice, a significant portion of the school counseling program involves group work, either in small groups or classroom sessions. There appears to be a strong rationale for such interventions. Therefore, it would seem appropriate to examine some of the special issues associated with approaching group work from a developmental perspective.

Topics and Competencies

Two of the most apparent uses of developmental theory in group work concern choices of topics and expectations regarding competencies. We would not expect that topics needed by 11th graders would be appropriate for 7-year-olds. Developmental theory, particularly understanding of developmental tasks, gives us a framework for anticipating when certain issues should be addressed. For example, some concerns related to human sexuality are dealt with as they become important to adolescents. Earlier presentation of the information might be wasted on "deaf ears" and would not reflect optimal timing. Specific suicide-prevention programs might be necessary for older adolescents. A more appropriate intervention in elementary schools would be promoting healthy self-esteem, rather than focusing on the suicide issue at all.

Using developmental theory as a framework for group interventions requires much more than determining scope and sequence, however. Practitioners need to use what they know about development effectively to design programs that anticipate issues and provide skills and information as a means of preventing problems from arising. If the interventions are in classrooms, the topics need to be integrated with the rest of the curriculum. Often students see the counselor only once a week or once every other week. Without connections being made to the rest of their world, or without clear objectives stated by the counselor, students are not sure what the visit was all about. They are left wondering, "Who was that masked man (woman or person!)?"

The choice of topics for classroom interventions or small groups must be based on what we know about where most of these children and adolescents are developmentally. We can assess what tasks they are most likely attempting to master, what crises they are attempting to resolve, what social issues the particular culture presents for them, and what structures they have in place for processing information. These structures may reflect reasoning in cognitive, ethical, or social domains. The tasks, crises, and social issues will guide us in selecting topics. The cognitive structures will assist us in choosing our methods. However, developmental theory also tells us that there is not an absolute age-to-stage correlation. Therefore, we can anticipate that not all sixth graders will be at the exact same place developmentally. Some will need more structure in activities, whereas others will test limits as they seek more independence. Counselors need to be able to "read and flex" in meeting these individual needs. An additional way to use the differences in developmental levels within any one classroom or small group is to encourage discussion. This discussion allows consolidation of stage change by those who are at higher levels and provokes growth for others by exposing them to a variety of perspectives.

As goals and objectives are determined, it is also important to consider student competencies. What do we expect children and adolescents to be able to do at certain ages and stages? Attention to this question can help us in the selection of both topics and methods. It can also help us evaluate the effects of our interventions. Can they do what we wanted them to be able to do? If not, we can regroup, plan other strategies, and try again. Evaluation related to stated objectives and competencies is essential and yet often disregarded in program implementation. We often function on a misguided notion of "feeling good" about what occurred, rather than really checking out our assumptions. Are the students really benefiting from our interventions? Although our long-term goal may be to promote development, other outcome measures are needed. These measures can be based on content presented or competencies expected.

Perhaps the easiest way to indicate how developmental theory should impact group interventions is to contrast what has traditionally occurred with what needs to happen. The important piece is that topics are not selected out of thin air or from the most current "hot topic," but from what we know about where these students are. Methods are not chosen randomly from a cookbook of strategies, but from what we know about how development occurs. Objectives are not isolated unit by unit, but are an integrated part of the whole school program. Activities are not selected to keep students busy or to give teachers a break, but for some real and identified purpose to meet a particular need. Goals are not determined one grade level at a time, but are strategically planned to encompass the entire educational experience. School counseling programs do not necessarily look exactly the same at every school because we know that development occurs within a context, and each of these contexts can be different. Geographic, social, and economic factors change the context, and therefore change the needs. The absolute bottom line to group intervention is still to promote the development of individual children and adolescents—to provide environments in which they can learn more complex methods of processing their experiences.

Classroom Interventions or Small Groups

In attempting to promote development, counselors are often faced with choices concerning the best intervention. Group work is no exception. Counselors must make professional judgment calls on which topics or issues will be dealt with through classroom interventions and which should be handled in small groups. Several factors need to be taken into consideration in making this decision: (a) your purpose, (b) the nature of the problem or issue, (c) the needs of the school, and (d) the developmental level of the students.

Your own purpose for an intervention and the nature of the particular problem or issue are related. In group work, counselors deal with sharing information, teaching skills to prevent problems, shaping new behaviors, enhancing development, and intervening in crisis. Some of these areas are better dealt with in small groups than classroom settings. The personal nature of some issues, such as dealing with family change, requires a more protected and confidential environment. Changing and enhancing particular behaviors are also easier in small-group settings because you have better opportunities for monitored practice and feedback. Providing support for identified at-risk students can be better conducted in small groups: More individualized attention can be provided to children and adolescents who rarely receive that attention in positive ways.

However, for sharing information or teaching skills for prevention, classroom interventions reach the largest number of students in the shortest amount of time and appear to be an effective approach. Some behavior-change programs, such as managing conflict, can also be very productively addressed in classrooms. These programs are usually preventive in nature and involve setting up a structure that the whole class accepts as an appropriate method for settling disputes.

The choice concerning crisis intervention in groups will largely depend on the nature and scope of what has occurred. Generally, you would limit involvement to those individuals directly involved in the crisis. This will usually mean working with a small group. Often, there is not a conscious choice for counselors in this situation. The students in crisis are simply "given" to the counselor or appear at the door all by themselves. This type of small group is usually not ongoing, but rather an example of brief or solution-focused counseling. However, sometimes the crisis does involve a whole class. In those cases, two possibilities exist. The first is to facilitate discussion of issues in a large group. The advantage of this approach is that there is no room for speculation about "who said what about whom and when." Everyone is hearing the same information and is a part of the same process. A second approach is to work initially in a series of small-group discussions to allow everyone to share feelings and perspectives. A class meeting would follow the small-group sessions. This approach allows a more thorough exploration of the situation, but also requires more of a time commitment on the part of the counselor and teacher.

The needs of the particular school also have to be addressed as decisions are made concerning small-group and classroom sessions. Some schools have very well-organized and effective teacher-advisory programs in place. The types of interventions that counselors might provide in classrooms are already being addressed by teachers. In those situations, use of a counselor's time might be more productively focused on small-group activities, with occasional classroom visits based on teacher request. In other situations, the issues most appropriately handled in small groups may not, for whatever reason, be apparent in a particular school setting. Hence, counselors would be more available for class sessions. Teachers and counselors may also decide to collaborate to offer certain topics in class as team teachers or to facilitate small-group discussions simultaneously. An additional possibility is for counselors to serve as consultants for classroom interventions, yet rarely deliver the services themselves. They would instead provide resources, information, and support for teachers carrying out activities.

Finally, in choosing between small-group and classroom sessions, consideration should be given to the type of school and the developmental level of the students. Generally speaking, classroom sessions are effective in working with elementary school students, whereas small groups are particularly powerful for middle school students. Children are usually still at a stage where information and skill building can be easily accommodated in systematic presentations. Children often still look to adults for structure and direction. On the other hand, adolescents are very attached to and interested in the perspectives and feelings of their peers. Small-group work allows for a greater depth and connection to those peers than a class session does. More attention can be provided by the facilitator to make sure those connections and relationships are enhanced and are appropriate for the school environment.

High school students could also greatly benefit from small-group experience. Unfortunately, the high school schedule often makes such opportunities infrequent. In fact, the same is true for classroom sessions. High school counselors generally are in classrooms only for academic and vocational-information sessions. One possibility for changing this may be in attempting to integrate counseling goals with existing curricula in English, health, or social studies. Counselors could then serve as facilitators of dilemma discussions based on literature assignments, guest speakers on conflict resolution, or special resources on the effects of mental health on physical health. (Although this approach is being given as a method for high school counselors having access to classrooms, the author's bias is that this integrated approach to education is actually the best system for children and adolescents K–12).

Choice of Materials

In conducting groups, counselors are faced with decisions concerning the specific materials to use, particularly in classroom sessions. There are a number of packaged programs in addition to individual activities of the counselor's own creation. In selecting packaged curricula, it is very important that counselors carefully evaluate the program and consider their own objectives for the classroom interventions.

Choosing materials without this careful evaluation process leaves counselors open to questions and criticisms from various populations. These external voices are best dealt with by having clear objectives supported by the accepted and established goals for the school counseling program. Counselors must have purposes for the activities, strategies, and programs they choose, and they must be prepared to explain those reasons. Using materials simply because they are fun or a part of a smartly packaged product is not good enough. The question must be asked, "Does the program or activity meet a specific school counseling-related objective or goal?" Having defensible rationales also prevents the necessity of abandoning very valuable and effective programs and strategies with the first wave of questions from more conservative consumers. Often when counselors can explain why they are using a particular approach, and anchor that reason in an appropriate counseling goal, the criticism fades to the background. However, when the counselor uses a program only because it was presented at a conference or was used by the counselor who was there before, the rationale is extremely weak, and the probability of the criticism flourishing is very strong.

Scheduling

As implied in an earlier section, scheduling is generally also an issue in planning small groups and classroom sessions. An important consideration for counselors is to remember the comprehensive nature of their programs. Group interventions represent only a portion of the school counseling program. Being scheduled in on the master schedule for classroom sessions is not appropriate when viewed with other expectations and responsibilities. Such a schedule locks too much time into the classroom component and does not offer the amount of flexibility needed to deal with crises. Completing periodic units, serving as a guest speaker or facilitator, or acting as a consultant to the classroom teachers makes a great deal more sense. When units are scheduled, it is important to remember what we know from developmental theory. Short-term approaches do not work in promoting development. Brief interventions are helpful for sharing information, but for promoting development continuity is needed. Being with a class for a full grading period or semester offers a greater chance for promoting development. During the next grading period, you could switch to other classes. This approach is much more beneficial than trying to meet every class every other week—a plan that often provides little consistency.

Small groups are generally easier to schedule in elementary and middle schools. In elementary schools, students are usually with the same teacher for the whole school day. Blocks of time that would be convenient for working with small groups of students from one class can be identified with the teacher's assistance. In middle schools, time is often set aside for interest classes that are very appropriately used for small groups. High schools offering study halls can also easily accommodate small-group interventions.

When study halls and interest classes are not available, counselors need to be a bit more creative in providing scheduling alternatives that do not intefere with academic efforts. Two of the most common alternatives are the floating and split-class schedules. The floating schedule involves changing the class period missed each week. For example, if running a six-week small-group intervention, a counselor might have the group meet the first week during first period, the second week during second period, and so on. In this way, the student misses any class only once in order to participate. Another option is to split the class time missed. In an example of this approach, the small group runs from the middle of first period through the middle of second period. This method allows students an opportunity to be there for a part of all of their classes. Some counselors also use a combination of these methods, splitting classes and floating times. An example of this approach would involve splitting time between first and second periods for three group sessions and between fifth and sixth periods for three sessions.

Scheduling options for classroom sessions and for small groups requires the cooperation of both administrators and classroom teachers. With such support, all types of intervention can be effectively scheduled and implemented. Without it, major obstacles exist to providing needed services. The importance of building collaborative and cooperative relationships cannot be overemphasized.

Components from Successful Programs to Promote Development

In planning classroom and small-group interventions, consideration of what we know about promoting development is extremely important. We can provide information, and even teach specific behaviors, in short-term interventions, but we cannot promote development with hit-or-miss approaches. The concepts of *continuity* and *integration* need to be central. Additionally, we need to provide balances of challenge and support in the units we develop. We also need to provide opportunities for significant role-taking experiences and reflection on those experiences. So what do these imperatives mean for practice?

One of the purposes for group interventions, particularly for classroom sessions, is to share information. Sharing information is possible in one session. We can explain the Scholastic Aptitude Test (SAT) or the application process for becoming a peer helper in one class. We cannot promote development or facilitate long-term behavior change in the same amount of time. Most of the research indicates that developmental change will not occur within even a 6-month period without specific interventions designed to promote development. As counselors, our best opportunity for promoting development is by collaborating with classroom teachers and truly integrating school counseling goals with academic curricula. This collaboration assists in providing continuity and a more authentic environment for development. The interventions can be a part of the bigger picture, and therefore an integrated portion of long-term intervention. In the past, counselors have tended to work in isolation and to separate their goals from the rest of the school program. Students often feel fractionalized—reduced to a collection of single subjects. It would be much more effective to work together and assist students in synthesizing content to make meaning of their lives.

We have also tended, in counseling, to offer much support and little challenge to students. If we are concerned about promoting development, we need to be engaged in offering both. Students need to be offered the opportunity to stretch in new ways, see new perspectives, and process experience in more complex patterns. In humanistic orientations to counseling, we always offer the opportunity to "pass" in activities. From a developmental perspective, we would certainly not force students to participate, but we would strongly encourage such involvement as a way of stretching. We would also provide support for that involvement. "I know this is difficult for you to try, but I am right here to help you figure out how to do it, if you need me." In planning group activities, counselors need to consider both of these components: (a) Have I built in enough challenge, a requirement for cognitive, ethical, or interpersonal stretching? and (b) Have I provided enough personal support for the students to attempt what seems a bit frightening to them? Have I let them know clearly that I am there for them . . . as a safety net?

The other components that are important in promoting development involve significant role taking and reflection. Meaningful role-taking experiences can be provided through opportunities for peer helping, peer tutoring, or participating in a service project. These opportunities allow students to take on new responsibilities and to expand their perspectives by being of assistance to others. Having these experiences is not enough, however. Students also need an opportunity to reflect on their actions. They need to process their feelings and share their ideas as a way of "owning" the growth. This reflection might occur in group sharing sessions or through journal writing.

A specific method for promoting development involves the use of dilemma discussion. Such discussions can easily be incorporated in classroom sessions or small-group work on almost any topic. Additionally, many dilemmas arise in the day-to-day lives of children and adolescents. Using these as "grist for the mill" can be particularly effective. As the facilitator of these discussions, it is particularly important to remember that students will be attracted to reasoning one level above their own modal stage. The counselor can make general assessments of levels of reasoning by listening to the discussion. If alternative approaches and rationales are not offerred by students, the facilitator can provide those ideas as a way to provoke thought. Choosing reasoning one level above and presenting a new option to students can precipitate cognitive dissonance or disequilibrium—a prerequisite for developmental change.

ASCA Materials

One very helpful resource for the "nuts and bolts" of conducting groups is available from the American School Counselor Association (ASCA). As a service to members, an in-service workshop (Coy, 1991) was developed to provide a practical guide for school counselors related to group work. The workshop was based on materials developed by Morganett (1990). The materials from ASCA provide a rationale for group counseling, steps in organizing the group experience, guidelines for success, and ethical considerations. The workshop also gives helpful information concerning who should be included in small-group interventions. Table 10 outlines the organizational steps taken from this model.

Summary

Group work, whether in small groups or classroom sessions, is an important part of a school counselor's role. There are several important factors for counselors to consider as they design, develop, and

TABLE 10
Organizing the Group Experience

1. Conduct needs assessment
2. Develop written proposal
3. Advertise the group
4. Obtain informed consent from parent/guardian
5. Conduct pregroup interview
6. Select group members
7. Administer pretest
8. Conduct sessions
9. Administer posttest
10. Follow-up and evaluation

Note. From *Group Counseling: A practical Guide for School Counselors* (p. 1) by D. R. Coy, 1991, Alexandria, VA: American School Counselors Association.

deliver this portion of their program. Developmental theory and principles can provide a framework for determining topics, goals, objectives, and competencies. Understanding how development occurs can also keep us from expecting short-term results or from conducting a school counseling program in isolation from the rest of the educational experience. If we are to truly provide environments for children and adolescents to develop more complex methods for processing their experiences, we will need to work collaboratively with others in long-term commitment.

CHAPTER 4

Working with Parents and Teachers

How can counselors use developmental theory in working with parents and teachers? Two significant possibilities exist. The first involves sharing developmental information about children and adolescents with adults. The second requires remembering that development is a lifelong process. Parents and teachers who walk into the counseling office are also at a particular stage of development in their own lives.

Sharing Developmental Information

Sharing information concerning development can assist parents and teachers in understanding the young people in their lives. Such understanding can promote setting realistic expectations. Sometimes adults can become very excited or troubled over certain behaviors (particularly from adolescents) that are actually very normal for the stage of development. Just knowing that the behavior is normal is often reassuring. In some cases, the adults may still need to take action, but at least they do not view the student as pathological. Instead, the children or adolescents may need guidelines or boundaries for appropriate behavior.

At other times, parents and teachers may need the information in order to identify actions that are not developmentally appropriate. Certain behaviors at particular stages are fairly clear signals for intervention. As mentioned in a previous chapter, an imaginary friend for a 6-year-old is not problematic. For a much older child, it would be. An adolescent who associates strictly with adults and has no identifiable peer group is very likely in need of some type of special assistance or opportunity for age-related interaction.

In sharing developmental information with parents and teachers, emphasis should be placed on individual variation within stages and the lack of rigid age-to-stage correlations. Although developmental theory provides a very helpful framework for understanding a process, stage descriptions will never match the true richness of spirit and "being" of an individual child or adolescent.

Adult Development

The second use for developmental theory in working with parents and teachers concerns their own continued development as adults. We are not "finished products" when we reach age 18. Instead, as Erikson initially described, we continue to develop across the life span.

Accepting this assumption means that the adults with whom we work will be at different stages of development also. Some will process information concretely, others abstractly. Some will need a great deal of structure in any situation or in any intervention they are asked to try with their child or student; others will need very little. Their behaviors will be motivated by different aspects of ethical reasoning. Some will want to please; others, to follow the rules; still others, to work for the "greatest good." What do these factors mean for counselors? Primarily, the meaning is that developmental assessment needs to be a part of the consultation process also. We need to consider in our interventions where the adults are in terms of their continued development. We can adapt our approaches based on the information.

In addition, we can consider opportunities to promote development for parents and teachers. A key component in developmental theory concerns the potential for growth that accompanies appropriate interaction between the individual and the environment. To assume that the adult years are devoid of new situations, dilemmas, and appropriate interactions that could promote growth is to belittle the human life experience. A number of theorists indicate that a great deal of "developmental work" remains to be done during adult years. The highest stages of development in various domains are rarely being achieved. Perhaps by providing opportunities for support and guided reflection, we can actually help promote the development of the parents and teachers with whom we work.

A Specific Application

A specific application of developmental concepts in consultation involves work with beginning teachers. If counselors can positively impact the development of teachers, they will in turn affect what goes on in the classroom for children and adolescents.

Sprinthall (personal communication, March, 1986) reframed Hunt's conceptual levels to reflect teacher attitudes toward learning and teaching. These stages are helpful in understanding how teacher development occurs, and indicate some of the differences that counselors might hear in working with first-year teachers.

Stage 1—There is strong evidence of concrete thinking. Knowledge is seen as fixed. Stage 1 teachers tend to employ a singular tried-and-true method, relying heavily on advance organizers. These individuals often see teaching as "filling the students up" with facts, and view learning as a compliant process. Generally, these teachers will offer only highly structured learning experiences, following the curriculum guide completely. Other tendencies include an inability to recognize or deal with student feelings, a reluctance to talk about their own inadequacies, and a lack of distinction between theory and fact. These teachers tend to stay at Bloom's Levels 1 and 2, regardless of the student's level.

Stage 2—There is a growing awareness of the difference between concrete and abstract thinking, with a corresponding ability to separate facts, opinions, and theories. Stage 2 teachers are able to employ different teaching models with some evidence of systematic matching and mismatching to vary structure and promote development. These teachers are open to new ideas and adaptations, sensitive to students' emotional needs, and appropriate in choices of evaluative criteria and methods. Stage 2 teachers also enjoy autonomy, value self-directed learning for themselves and their students, and employ Bloom's Levels 1–4 when appropriate.

Stage 3—Stage 3 teachers understand knowledge as a process of successive approximations, show originality in adapting innovations in the classroom to meet student needs, and are comfortable in applying all appropriate teaching models. They respond sensitively to the emotional needs of students, have a high tolerance for frustration and ambiguity, and can match and mismatch with expert flexibility. Although these teachers can stay on task despite major distractions, they also ask questions rather than automatically comply with directions. Stage 3 teachers foster intensive questioning by students, use all of Bloom's levels appropriately, teach both content and feeling, and use careful and objective criteria in evaluation.

An additional helpful framework in understanding the needs of first-year teachers was developed by Fuller in 1969. Fuller described a developmental conceptualization of the concerns of beginning teachers. She based her description on interviews with numerous first-year educators. Fuller identified three stages of anxiety or concern: (a) the preteaching phase or nonconcern, (b) the early teaching phase or concern for self, and (c) the later teaching phase or concern for students. The preteaching phase centers on lack of awareness. Prior to entering a classroom and taking over full responsibility, it is difficult to have a real understanding of what the tasks and issues are. The early teaching phase concerns center around self-protection, self-adequacy, class control, and subject-matter adequacy. Finding a place in the power structure and understanding the expectations of supervisors, principals, and parents also appear to be important considerations in the early phase of teaching. The student portion of the sequence can best be seen as a set of qualitatively different issues centering on student learning, student progress, and, most significantly, ways in which a teacher might implement this progress. Fuller suggested that resolution of the early stages of concern would allow these more student-oriented issues to emerge.

Based on this suggestion, and because of the very nature of the first year of teaching, beginning teachers provide an excellent target population for staff development to promote growth. Two of the components previously discussed that are associated with successful interventions are already in place for beginning teachers: significant role taking and challenge. Teaching involves the extraordinary challenge of providing environments and experiences in which a child may learn more fully what it means to be human. To ensure the appropriate provision of these environments and experiences for children, special attention must be given to the process of growth and continued development for teachers. A staff development program designed to offer support and an opportunity to reflect on their experiences would appear to be beneficial. Counselors could be ideal providers of such services.

Counselor-Led Support Groups

Counselor-led support groups allow beginning teachers to share their concerns, feelings, and experiences with each other. These groups have been recommended as innovative counselor interventions (Gerler, 1992), and have been shown to be successful in promoting growth in participants from concern about self to concern about students (Herring, 1989; Paisley, 1990).

In keeping with our knowledge concerning successful interventions, work with beginning teachers should not involve an isolated group meeting. Instead, beginning teachers should have an opportunity to participate in a small group led by a counselor over the course of at least one semester. Groups should meet approximately twice a month for 1½ hours. The group meetings need to be confidential and in no way associated with the beginning teachers' evaluations.

Counselors are natural leaders for such discussion groups based on their training in group process and facilitation. The counselor's role in these groups would involve guiding and directing discussion, posing questions or topics concerning their experiences, and modeling the components of effective communication. Counselors can also facilitate the clarification of feelings concerning experiences and help in generating alternative approaches to problem solving. As in any group, some monitoring of the discussion will also be necessary to ensure that all participants will be able to share their concerns.

Leading these groups will give counselors special insights into the needs of beginning teachers. With their permission, the counselors can serve as advocates with school administrators. This advocacy can be carried out in general terms without threat to individual confidentiality. Counselors can also provide and clarify information from administration to beginning teachers concerning general policies and programs. Such information serves an important orientation need for first-year professionals. Most importantly, counselors can listen and observe in an effort to understand the current developmental level and stage of concern. Using appropriate support and challenge or matching and mismatching, counselors can attempt to provide the experiences and the environment that will promote development.

What is the real purpose of these beginning teacher support groups? The groups will provide a format for first-year teachers to process concerns that they experience at particular points in time and to allow for guided reflection about those concerns. The groups will provide for group bonding and support so that participants will feel encouraged to share concerns and experiences with each other, practice active listening with their colleagues, and develop self-confidence in their new professional roles. Thoroughly exploring feelings and experiences will allow resolution of the early stages of concern that are more egocentric and will encourage the beginning teachers to become more focused on students (Fuller, 1969). The groups may also alleviate stress, prevent burnout, and allow schools to retain teachers who sometimes leave the field due to inadequate support systems (Paisley, 1987).

The First Session

During the first session, the ground rules for participation need to be established by the groups. These usually include such topics as confidentiality, punctuality in beginning and ending times, and respect for individual differences. Expectations and goals concerning group participation also need to be discussed. The counselor/leader needs to clearly outline the purpose of the group during this first session. Beginning teachers need to be assured that their comments will in no way affect their evaluations.

The remainder of the first session can be used for introductions and get-acquainted activities. These might include sharing of names, backgrounds, and initial concerns as teachers. Basic information about active listening might also be presented at this time.

The last few minutes of group can be used to share positive experiences as educators that have occurred during the preceding weeks. This allows the session to end on a positive note, to indicate an interest in areas other than those associated with problems, and to encourage a positive focus for the upcoming weeks.

Succeeding Sessions

The remaining sessions for the group can follow an informal discussion group format. The first portion of the group should be used to process immediate concerns, information items, or leftover agenda items from previous meetings. The main segment of time should be devoted to current concerns or experiences presented by beginning teachers for feedback or ventilation. Sometimes the counselor/leader may choose to pose questions for reflection. The final few minutes of group can be used for any reminders concerning the next group meeting and for sharing positive experiences as educators.

Guided Reflection

Periodically, questions can be posed in an interview format by the counselor/leader. These questions are designed to stimulate discussion and to promote reflection on the teaching experience. Some examples of these questions include:

> What concerns you most right now as an educator?
> What are your greatest challenges as an educator?
> How have you dealt with those challenges?
> What resources are available to you in meeting these challenges?
> How do you feel about your decision to become a teacher?
> At this point, what do you feel your strengths are as a teacher?
> In self-evaluation, what area do you think you need to work on as a teacher?
> How has teaching been different from and similar to your expectations?

(These questions were suggested by an individual interview used in research by the Research Center on Teacher Education.)

Beginning teachers can also be encouraged to use journal writing as an additional method for reflection on experience. The use of a journal allows participants another outlet for ventilation of feelings and processing of experiences.

Potential Benefits

There are numerous potential benefits from counselor-led support groups for beginning teachers. The first year of teaching is an extremely stressful and hectic one. Many teachers are not only adjusting to career responsibilities, but are also making a transition from full-time student to participant in the world of work. Without appropriate support systems, many potentially good teachers will leave the field.

We should also not underestimate the ripple effect that intervening with teachers will have for students. Because most counselors face extremely high ratios as they deliver services, direct contact with all students on any regular basis is impossible. Teachers see these students and interact with them daily. If counselors can have a more positive impact on the development of teachers and alleviate at least some of the stress that they face, then children in classrooms may well be the beneficiaries.

In fact, research has indicated that teachers at higher stages of development are more adaptive in teaching styles (tolerant, flexible), more responsive to individual differences, more empathic, and more accurate in reading and responding to emotions. In short, teachers at higher stages of development function in ways that are more complex and more consistent with concepts of effective teaching (Oja & Sprinthall, 1978).

Beyond the benefits for the individual teachers and the children whom they teach, counselor-led support groups can also help improve relationships between teachers and counselors. Participating beginning teachers develop a personal relationship with a counselor and have a better understanding of the counselor role. Some of the misconceptions and walls are broken down, making future consultation and collaboration much easier.

Summary

In addition to being of assistance in our work with children and adolescents, developmental theory can also provide helpful information for use in consultation. Sharing developmental characteristics with parents and teachers can improve their understanding of their children and students. Using what we know about adult development can offer a framework for our understanding of the stage of the parent or teacher. We can adapt interventions accordingly or design programs to actually promote development. The beginning teacher support group, outlined in this chapter, is presented only as an example of such an intervention. Creative counselors will be able to design and implement numerous programs based on developmental concepts that will be of great benefit to parents and teachers.

REFERENCES FOR PART ONE

Allen, J. (1988). *Inscapes of a child's world: Jungian approaches to therapy.* Dallas, TX: Spring.

Anderson, J. (1987). *PUMSY: In pursuit of excellence.* Eugene, OR: Timberline Press.

Axline, V. (1947). *Play therapy.* Boston: Houghton-Mifflin.

Axline, V. (1964). *Dibs: In search of self.* Boston: Houghton-Mifflin.

Carkhuff, R. R. (1972). *The art of helping: A guide for developing skills for parents, teachers, and counselors.* Amherst, MA: Human Resources Development Press.

Coy, D. R. (1991). Group counseling: A practical guide for school counselors [An in-service workshop outline]. Alexandria, VA: American School Counselor Association.

Ellis, A. (1962). *Reason and emotion in psychotherapy.* New York: Lyle Stuart.

Erikson, E. (1963). *Childhood and society.* New York: W. S. Norton.

Fuller, F. (1969). Concerns of teachers: A developmental conceptualization. *American Educational Research Journal, 6,* 207–266.

Gilligan, C. (1982). *In a different voice.* Cambridge, MA: Harvard University Press.

Ginzberg, E., Ginsburg, S., Axelrad, S., & Herma, J. L. (1951). *Occupational choice: An approach to general theory.* New York: Columbia Press.

Glosoff, H., & Koprowicz, C. (1990). *Children achieving potential: An introduction to elementary school counseling and state-level policies.* Alexandria, VA: American Association for Counseling and Development.

Gordon, T. (1974). *T.E.T.: Teacher effectiveness training.* New York: David McKay Company.

Havighurst, R. J. (1972). *Developmental tasks and education* (3rd ed.). New York: David McKay.

Herring, R. (1989). *Psychological maturity and teacher education: A comparison of interactional models for preservice teachers.* Unpublished doctoral dissertation, North Carolina State University, Raleigh.

Hunt, D. E. (1975). Person-environment interaction: A challenge found wanting before it was tried. *Review of Educational Research, 45,* 209–230.

Hunt, D. E. (1978). Theorists are persons, too: On preaching what you practice. In C. Parker (Ed.), *Encouraging student development in college.* Minneapolis: University of Minnesota Press.

Kohlberg, L. (1969). Stage and sequence: The cognitive developmental approach to socialization. In D. Goslin (Ed.), *Handbook of socialization theory and research* (pp. 347–480). Chicago: Rand-McNally.

Kottman, T., & Warlick, J. (1989). Adlerian play therapy: Practical considerations. *Individual Psychology: The Journal of Adlerian Theory, Research, and Practice, 45,* 433–446.

Landreth, G. (1991). *Play therapy: The art of the relationship.* Muncie, IN: Accelerated Development.

Morganett, R. S. (1990). *Skills for living: Group counseling activities for young adolescents.* Champaign, IL: Research Press.

Oaklander, V. (1977). *Windows to our children.* Highland, NY: The Center for Gestalt Development.

Oja, S., & Sprinthall, N. (1978). Psychological and moral development for teachers. In N. A. Sprinthall & R. L. Mosher (Eds.), *Value development as the aim of education* (pp. 117–134). Schenectady, NY: Character Research Press.

Paisley, P. O. (1987). *The developmental effects of a staff development program for beginning teachers.* Unpublished doctoral dissertation, North Carolina State University, Raleigh.

Paisley, P. O. (1990). Counseling involvement in promoting the developmental growth of beginning teachers. *The Journal of Humanistic Education and Development, 29*(1), 20–31.

Piaget, J. (1950). *The psychology of intelligence.* New York: Harcourt, Brace & Company.

Rogers, C. R. (1942). *Counseling and psychotherapy.* Boston: Houghton-Mifflin.

Selman, R. (1980). *The growth of interpersonal understanding.* New York: Academic Press.

Sprinthall, N. A., & Collins, W. A. (1988). *Adolescent psychology: A developmental view.* New York: McGraw-Hill.

Sprinthall, N. A., & Thies-Sprinthall, L. (1983). The teacher as adult learner: A cognitive developmental view. In G. Griffin (Ed.), *Staff development* (pp. 13–35). Chicago: National Society for the Study of Education.

Sprinthall, R. C., & Sprinthall, N. A. (1981). *Educational psychology: A developmental approach.* Reading, MA: Addison-Wesley.

Super, D. (1972). Vocational development theory: Persons, positions, and processes. In J. M. Whitely & A. Resmikoff (Eds.), *Perspectives on vocational development.* Washington, DC: American Personnel and Guidance Association.

Thompson, C. L., & Rudolph, L. B. (1992). *Counseling children* (3rd ed.). Pacific Grove, CA: Brooks/Cole.

Tiedeman, D. V., & O'Hara, R. P. (1963). *Career development: Choice and adjustment.* Princeton, NJ: College Entrance Examination Board.

Winnett, B. R., Bornstein, P., Cogswell, K., & Paris, A. (1987). Cognitive–behavioral therapy for childhood depression: A levels-of-treatment approach. *Journal of Child and Adolescent Psychotherapy, 4*, 283–286.

Zunker, V. (1990). *Career counseling: Applied concepts of life planning* (3rd ed.). Pacific Grove, CA: Brooks/Cole.

PART TWO

SAMPLE DEVELOPMENTAL PROGRAMS

Introduction to Part Two

Part Two outlines four programs using the developmental principles discussed in Part One. As school counselors attempt to implement comprehensive developmental programs, theory must be translated into practice. These programs are offered as examples of the type of theoretically sound interventions that the authors recommend. These programs were originally published as articles in *The School Counselor* and *Elementary School Guidance and Counseling*.

In individual counseling, the developmental level of students in various domains can provide guidelines for conceptualizing issues, choosing approaches, and adapting strategies. As an example, in chapter 5, Parr and Ostrovsky outline specific strategies and approaches for use in individual counseling based on Kohlberg's stages of moral reasoning. The authors suggest counseling strategies based on preconventional and conventional ethical reasoning. The strategies are calibrated according to the stage of moral development.

In small-group counseling or classroom guidance, programs must be designed to meet the criteria associated with successful developmental interventions. These programs must be offered over a sufficient length of time to facilitate change, and must provide a balance of challenge and support as well as an opportunity for reflection. Successful programs build on these components as well as opportunities for role-taking, dilemma discussion, and plus-one reasoning or modeling.

The authors of the articles represented in chapters 6–8 describe such successful group interventions designed to promote development. The interventions in these chapters are thoroughly outlined so that practitioners may replicate these programs. Additionally, research findings that validate the effectiveness of the interventions are presented.

At the elementary level, Borders and Paisley (chapter 6) provide a classroom guidance intervention using quality children's literature. Children are given an opportunity to hear stories for several months, discuss their responses to the experience, and relate through journals their own connections to the conflicts or situations faced by characters. Quality stories provide dilemmas and opportunities for secondary role taking, whereas class discussions allow students to hear the reasoning of classmates at various levels of development.

At the middle school level, a peer counseling program for students experiencing divorce is described by Sprinthall, Hall, and Gerler (chapter 7). In this program, high school students became peer counselors for groups of middle school students. The program was designed using developmental constructs from Loevinger, Kohlberg, and Selman. The developmental concepts of role taking and plus-one reasoning were specifically incorporated. High school students "took on the role" of peer helper to younger students. Middle school students were provided with slightly older peers as "plus-one models."

With high school students, an intervention using dilemma discussion in drug-abuse prevention is outlined by Paisley, Gerler, and Sprinthall (chapter 8). This program was based particularly on the use of dilemma discussion suggested by the work of Kohlberg in moral development and Selman in interpersonal understanding. Drug-related dilemmas were used to promote discussion to challenge students' reasoning and provide a secondary role-taking experience through hearing the insights of peers.

The four chapters in Part Two provide examples of the necessary translation of theory into practice that can be used in school counseling programs. The suggested interventions are each based on developmental principles and concepts. School counselors can use these sample programs as models for: (a) adapting individual counseling based on stages of development in other domains, or (b) planning and implementing small-group or classroom guidance programs to promote development in various content areas.

CHAPTER 5

The Role of Moral Development in Deciding How to Counsel Children and Adolescents

Gerald D. Parr and Mary Ostrovsky

Although Lawrence Kohlberg's work on moral development first appeared as an unpublished doctoral dissertation in the late 1950s, his ideas seem to have had little impact on the literature regarding school counseling. Most of the major theories that have influenced school counseling (e.g., Roger's person-centered theory or Glasser's reality therapy) do not feature developmental issues as important in planning intervention strategies. Developmental issues are discussed in several theories of family therapy (e.g., Haley, 1973), but these theories stress developmental tasks rather than developmental stages per se. There have been, however, several articles on the application of Kohlberg's ideas to moral education. For example, Wasserman, working in collaboration with Kohlberg (Kohlberg & Wasserman, 1980), reported an innovative, and apparently successful, model of moral education, which attempted to foster a schoolwide atmosphere favor-

---

This chapter is taken directly from Parr, G.D., & Ostrovsky, M. (1991). The role of moral development in deciding how to counsel children and adolescents. *The School Counselor, 39*(1), 14–19.

able to moral development. Wasserman's approach included the formation of committees to resolve conflicts, to establish school policies, and to sponsor school projects and programs (including interpersonal skills training for peer counselors and advisors). A steady stream of research articles, most of which support Kohlberg's basic tenets, have also appeared. Gibbs (1977), for example, in his constructive critique of Kohlberg's work, concluded that the first four stages of Kohlberg's hierarchy were well supported by research and were conceptually consistent with Piagetian theory.

Though sparse in numbers, articles relating to Kohlberg's concepts of moral development to the counseling profession have appeared in recent years. Bradley (1985), for example, found that a 4-month counseling program aimed at facilitating moral development for ex-offenders led to a substantial increase in moral development scores on the Defining Issues Test (Rest, 1980). The intervention in this study consisted of 1 hour of individual counseling and 3 hours of group counseling per week, during which the ex-offenders viewed and then discussed moral dilemmas from the *Values of Democracy Series* filmstrips. Moral development has been positively related to counseling experience and training (Welfel & Lipsitz, 1983) and to helper empathy (Bowman & Reeves, 1987). Ivey (1980) has argued for a value-centered advocacy model as a viable and needed role for the school counselor. The thrust of these and similar articles nevertheless fails to provide the school counselor with guidelines for how to use the knowledge on moral development when working with children in a typical school setting. This article attempts to fill that void by providing a framework wherein commonly used counseling techniques can be tailored and refined to match the client's stage of moral development.

Stages of Moral Development

Kohlberg's theory parallels Piaget's theory. One key tenet is that moral development progresses sequentially. Another is that a person thinks and behaves somewhat consistently within one stage, and that experiences are most meaningful when they synchronize with a person's developmental readiness. Thus, in anticipation of what will follow, the counselor should ask: How can I tailor my interventions to be responsive to my client's developmental readiness? Recognizing the importance of client readiness is clearly evident in many counseling theories; for example, the behaviorist shaped behavior by successive approximation (Comier & Comier, 1985), and the neurolinguistic programmer calibrates interventions to match the client's frame of reference (Bandler & Grinder, 1982).

The stages that follow delineate client readiness in terms of moral development. Each stage is named, with the approximate ages associated with that stage, followed by a brief description (Kohlberg & Wasserman, 1980).

Preconventional Level

Stage One: punishment-and-obedience orientation (5 to 7 years of age). This child is responsive to consequences and deferential to power but lacks an appreciation of the values behind rules and authority.

Stage Two: instrumental-relativist orientation (8 to 12 years of age). This child is pragmatic, approaching others with a set of "you scratch my back, I'll scratch yours" values; loyalty, fairness, and justice are not, at this point, ideals that influence actions.

Conventional Level

Stage Three: interpersonal concordance or good boy-nice girl orientation (13 to 16 years of age). This adolescent is guided by an attempt to conform to shared norms of what is right. For the first time, behavior is frequently judged by its intention (e.g., "he means well").

Stage Four: law and order orientation (16 years of age and over). This adolescent respects social order for its own sake and will behave well out of a sense of duty.

Postconventional, Autonomous, or Principled Level

Stage Five: the social-contract legalistic orientation (adult). At this level, the individual is aware of the relativism of personal values and opinions. Unlike stage four, where an individual is locked into a single view of right and wrong, an individual in this stage is concerned about the process whereby consensual agreement regarding legal and right behavior is reached.

Stage Six: The universal-ethical-principled orientation (adult). At this stage, one's sense of ethics is individually determined and guided by universal considerations of justice, of reciprocity, and of equality of human rights. Respect for the dignity of all human beings guides one's conscience.

Moral Stages and Counseling Strategies

The most basic and important principle that should guide the counselor's selection of an intervention, as noted earlier, is that counseling interventions should synchronize with the client's developmental readiness and personal idiosyncrasies. This synchronization allows the counselor to use the client's developmental and personal characteristics to promote and direct desired change. The following section delineates how counseling strategies can be calibrated according to stages of moral development.

Preconventional Level

In stage one, typically early elementary school age, children usually respond favorably to well-designed behavior management plans; token economies, for example, often work well. Most defer to teachers who exhibit appropriate assertiveness. Emotionally, these children need to feel that they have a place in the classroom and that it is a safe place. Thus, a behavior management plan must truly operate on the basis of successive approximations (i.e., the plan's design is such that every child can and does "win"); likewise, the teacher must avoid interacting with the children in either an aggressive or a passive manner. The counselor's role in this regard is that of a consultant who designs the behavior management plan and helps the teacher find ways to exercise authority that neither intimidates the children by being aggressive, nor confuses children by being too passive or unstructured.

Remembering that preconventional (stage one) children typically have not internalized values associated with appropriate behaviors, the counselor must be prepared to support the child, the teacher, and the parent when a behavior management plan's effectiveness falters. That support should come in the form of redefining a setback as something that is common and salvageable, rather than as something that indicates failure or lack of goodwill. The counselor assists the teacher-parent-child team by reviewing the plan for possible revisions. Some reinforcers, for example, lose their effectiveness over time and need to be replaced with alternatives. Change agents (parents and teachers) can become lax in carrying out their part of the agreement once a crisis has passed and the child's behavior has improved. Reinforcers may have been thinned too quickly, or the plan may not have made adequate provision for the pairing of primary reinforcers (e.g., food) with secondary reinforcers (e.g., praise). The teacher or parent may be having second thoughts about using a behavior management plan; some teachers complain that they haven't enough time to keep up with individual plans, and some parents may fear that "bribery" will not be beneficial to the child in the long run. The counselor draws upon basic listening skills and allows the teacher and parent to voice their concerns. The counselor may want to reassure the parents that their child will learn to value the target behavior for its own sake in time, and that supporting behavior with consequences at this age is not unusual or harmful. Talking it out is often sufficient—once the air is cleared, the plan can be examined, perhaps revised, and executed again.

Working with a child whose moral development has reached stage two of the preconventional level builds upon the former stage but shifts the focus to interpersonal relationships, especially peer relationships. The children by this time have come to emphasize peer relationships, and school counselors are often called upon to resolve conflicts that grow out of jealousy, transient alliances, broken promises, gossip, and competition for prizes and romantic pledges. Ideals such as fairness, loyalty, and justice are, at this point, beyond the child's grasp, so the counselor helps by appealing to the child's pragmatic sensibilities.

Conflict resolution with children of this age focuses on the costs that the conflict imposes on both parties and on specific ways that both can exit the conflict while saving face. The steps of conflict resolution include the following: first, allow both children to express their feelings and thoughts; second, help each child to understand the perspective of the other (active listening and role reversal at a basic level help to accomplish this perspective taking); third, ask each child to identify what costs have accrued as a result of the conflict (e.g., hurt feelings and perhaps the loss of a friendship); fourth, reframe the conflict as a mutual problem shared by both parties (i.e., have both children see that their needs are linked to each other's needs and that a solution will require a joint effort [note how this uses this child's pragmatic frame of reference]); fifth, have each child verbalize a commitment to resolve the conflict; sixth, have each child state to the other forgiveness over past hurts; seventh, brainstorm what actions each child might take to effect a solution to the problem; eighth, obtain an agreement about which alternative courses of action seem most feasible; ninth, seal the agreement by a contract (written or verbal); and last, discuss a follow-up plan if the agreement fails to work.

Although American classrooms emphasize individual rather than group achievement, preconventional, stage-two children can become quite motivated to help their peers when contingencies are defined in terms of group performance. The counselor could consult with teachers on forming groups and defining positive consequences for that group based on a minimal level of performance by every member of that group. Such an arrangement will tend to encourage peer tutoring and cooperation.

Counselors who work with children of this age on specific problems should define consequences in broader terms than when working with younger, stage-one children. Telephone privileges, for example, are very potent and durable reinforcers, because they support this child's emerging social needs and because the child rarely satiates of receiving or making calls to many different friends. Older children often resist agreeing to contingencies such as privileges, because they view them as fundamental rights that should not have to be earned. Thus, the importance of taking moral development into account when designing an intervention strategy is clear: With the preoperational child, a privilege is often an effective contingency because of its utilitarian value, whereas with the conventional child, attempting to influence change by such a contingency may evolve into a power struggle, because the adolescent sees such an arrangement as unfair.

Conventional Level

The adolescent of junior-high age is consumed with concern about conforming to peer norms. "Preppies" strain family budgets by demanding designer clothes; "stoners" strain the legal system as well as parents by demanding designer drugs. Parents can age quickly during their children's early teenage years, because the adolescent is emotionally labile; in the eyes of the adolescent, adults never seem to understand. What the adolescent means by this common complaint is, of course, that adults do not share or understand adolescent rules and values. A typical failure to reach adolescents occurs when a parent or helper says, "Don't worry what they think, just do what you know is right." This admonishment falls on deaf ears; it fails to match the adolescent's frame of reference.

Peer norms must be taken into account, then, when working with the conventional (stage three) adolescent. Group counseling can be quite effective. Basically, the counselor strikes a bargain with the group members; the counselor agrees to respect and understand their norms, and the group members agree to try out new norms (or existing norms redefined), which the counselor introduces as necessary conditions within the group (e.g., empathic listening to others, constructive confrontation of others, nondefensive exploration in response to confrontation, and appropriate self-disclosure [Egan, 1973]). Counselors can use the adolescent's orientation in individual work as well. To illustrate, the authors were asked to find a way to help an eighth-grade girl who physically attacked her peers three to four times a week. In talking with this girl, Bess, who was at best only an average student in a school of above average students, it became clear that her anger centered on a feeling that she could never fit into the norms of her peers. She further asserted that she may not be liked, but that she would never be ignored. So, our task, as we saw it, was to find a way that she could channel her personal goal for leadership and her developmental need for conformity toward an outlet that was more constructive than fighting. After some thought, we approached her teachers with a proposal in which we were to obtain her agreement to try out for the cheerleading squad, and the teachers who selected the cheerleaders in this school were to give her a real fighting chance to be selected. Bess was reluctant to try out, but after a mild challenge to her courage to take such a risk (note how this paced with her aggressive style), Bess went to tryouts. The teachers, cautious but desperate, selected her to be a ninth-grade cheerleader. Bess participated in only two fights during her ninth-grade year.

Adolescents in stage four, typically in high school, are loyal not only to their peer groups but also to causes. Their values have begun to crystalize, and they can be very vocal advocates of an issue. They love to debate issues, especially with adults, who are now viewed as worthy opponents or potential mentors. Beliefs are often rigidly cherished. These adolescents seem to want certainty as they face independent living in an adult world.

The zeal of these adolescents' convictions can disarm the school counselor, who may quickly forget, for example, that advice giving is usually an ill-fated helping strategy. The helping paradigm remains the same as with previous stages: synchronize the counseling intervention with the student's stage of development. Synchronization at this stage means encouraging adolescents to consider their convictions or decisions from every angle. For example, consider the 17-year-old girl who has decided to quit high school to marry her 21-year-old boyfriend. The counselor might project the consequences of this decision by using a Gestalt imagined-dialogue technique:

Counselor: "Mary, I would like to hear more about your plans to marry John. Would you be willing to sit in this chair and imagine what life will be like ten years from now if you do marry John now?"

(Later in the session) Counselor: "Ok, now sit in this chair, and imagine that you don't marry John now."

The counselor uses prompts while Mary considers her options. For example, after first allowing Mary to consider the blissful prospects of marrying John now, the counselor asks, "And if John continues to drink heavily each night after your marriage, what then? And if, though unplanned, you have children and John loses his job at the mill, what then?"

With this approach, the counselor avoids arguing with clients, which usually only presses them to further entrench themselves in their decision. The approach also avoids advice giving, which is usually ignored by clients. By contrast, the counselor using the approach in our example triggers client exploration rather than resistance. The counselor might conclude the session with Mary by suggesting that she talk over these matters with her boyfriend, who, it might be suggested, could demonstrate good faith by giving up his nightly six-pack for a few weeks (his response to that suggestion might provoke Mary's reexamination of her decision far more dramatically than a direct challenge by the counselor).

Conclusions

Understanding developmental stages can help school counselors tailor their strategies to address the special needs of their clients. Effective strategies synchronize with the developmental readiness of the client. Failure to take the developmental readiness into account can result in interventions that are poorly fitted to the client (i.e., the interventions may sabotage rapport with the client, may be so foreign to the client's frame of reference as to be meaningless, or may evoke resistance, which only aggravates the client's inappropriate behavior or hopelessness).

Mismatches between intervention and client readiness are perhaps too common. Token economies may effect desired change in the second grader but fail miserably with an eighth grader whose peers disapprove of working for a teacher's approval. Similarly, having a fourth grader consider the pros and cons of an interpersonal conflict in the abstract via a Gestalt chair technique may be misspent energy, whereas a pragmatic agreement between the affected parties may bring a swift and lasting resolution of the conflict.

Research on enhancing counselor effectiveness through achieving better matches between the counselor's choice of intervention and the client's developmental readiness is lacking. The complexity of the topic, with all the other factors that influence therapeutic outcome, makes researching this topic very difficult. The challenge to be more effective as practitioners exists in spite of this, and increasing one's awareness of stages of moral development may enhance clinical judgment and provide the basis for further research in this area.

References

Bandler, R., & Grinder, J. (1982). *Reframing: Neurolinguistic programming and the transformation of meaning*. Moab, UT: Real People Press.

Bowman, J. T., & Reeves, T. G. (1987). Moral development and empathy in counseling. *Counselor Education and Supervision, 26*(4), 293–298.

Bradley, L. J. (1985). Moral development of ex-offenders: Facts and findings. *Journal of Offender Counseling, 6*(1), 18–24.

Comier, W. L., & Comier, L. S. (1985). *Interviewing strategies for helpers: Fundamental skills and cognitive behavioral interventions*. Belmont CA: Brooks/Cole.

Egan, G. (1973). *Face to face: The small-group experience and interpersonal growth*. Belmont, CA: Brooks/Cole.

Gibbs, J. C. (1977). Kohlberg's stages of moral judgment: A constructive critique. *Harvard Educational Review, 47*(1), 43–61.

Haley, J. (1973). *Uncommon therapy*. New York: Norton.

Ivey, A. E. (1980). The counselor as psychoeducational consultant: Toward a value-centered advocacy model. *The Personnel and Guidance Journal, 58*(9), 567–577.

Kohlberg, L., & Wasserman, E. R. (1980). The cognitive developmental approach and the practicing counselor: An opportunity for counselors to rethink their roles. *The Personnel and Guidance Journal, 58*(9), 559–567.

Rest, J. R. (1980). Moral judgment research and the cognitive-developmental approach to moral education. *The Personnel and Guidance Journal, 58*(9), 602–605.

Welfel, E. R., & Lipsitz, N. E. (1983). Moral reasoning of counselors: Its relationship to level of training and counseling experience. *Counseling and Values, 27*, 194–203.

CHAPTER 6

Children's Literature as a Resource for Classroom Guidance

Sarah Borders and Pamela O. Paisley

Bibliotherapy is defined as a process or activity designed to help individuals solve problems or better understand themselves through their response to literature or media (Bodart, 1980). It consists of reading, viewing, or hearing of material, followed by a discussion led by a facilitator. The therapy takes place during this dynamic interaction between the reader and literature.

During the last 20 years, researchers and practitioners from the fields of counseling and library science have contributed valuable resources related to bibliotherapy. These resources suggest that bibliotherapy is a valuable tool for use with elementary school students. Although Baruth and Philips (1976) suggested that "bibliotherapy has enormous possibilities in school counseling" (p. 191), their focus was primarily problem-oriented and preventive. In a review of research, Schrank (1982) concluded that bibliotherapy is effective for attitude changes, mental health, self-concept development, and fear reduction. Schrank noted that "from kindergarten throughout one's formal years of schooling,

---

This chapter is taken directly from Borders, S., & Paisley, P.O. (1992). Children's literature as a resource for classroom guidance. *Elementary School Guidance & Counseling, 27*(2), 131–139.

books have always been a mainstay, a potential tool, for organizing discussion about personal, social, education and vocational development" (p. 224). Bibliotherapy has been shown additionally to have positive effects on students' problem-solving ability, prosocial behavior, values development, interpersonal relations, acceptance of people different from themselves, and reading achievement (Cornett & Cornett, 1980).

These studies along with "personal testimonies about the effects of certain books" (Cornett & Cornett, 1980, p. 15) support the claim that literature can promote developmental growth in a number of domains. Child psychiatrist Robert Coles (1989) has explored in his qualitative research the ways children's moral and ethical values develop. He has presented literature and art as important because they have the capacity to provide the "moral imagination" that can enhance growth. Experts from the field of library science, such as Judith Rovenger (1988), have pointed to certain literary selections with a special capacity to provide "ethical nourishment" and the universal eloquence to time release their messages.

The review of literature implies that bibliotherapy has possibilities beyond problem-centered interventions involving individual or small group counseling on specific topics. As the school counselor's role becomes increasingly associated with developmental programming (ASCA, 1978; Myrick, 1987), bibliotherapeutic approaches can also provide a wealth of resources for classroom guidance.

This study examined the developmental effects of a bibliotherapy-based classroom guidance curriculum. For the experimental group, titles were selected using criteria for quality developed by experts from the field of children's literature. The control group participated in an equal number of lessons selected from age-appropriate guidance curricula currently used by school counselors.

Method

Participants

This study was conducted during the spring semester of 1990 with two elementary school classes in a suburban North Carolina school district. The experimental group ($n = 22$) was a fourth- and fifth-grade combination. The control group ($n = 20$) was a fifth-grade class. Both were heterogeneously grouped.

Groups for the study were selected by the researcher based on principal recommendation. Teachers of the two groups were perceived by the principal to have similar teaching styles, and to be receptive to the guidance intervention. Both teachers employed a regular practice of reading aloud for pleasure for 20 to 30 minutes each day. Some grouping was done by the teachers in both classes for reading instruction, and all students had participated in the novel studies used by the fifth grade that year. Groups were similar in ability and racial and cultural makeup.

Procedures

The Paragraph Completion Test (Hunt, Greenwood, Noy, & Watson, 1973) was given to the children in both groups in January. The test was administered by the researcher and scored by a trained rater. A blind procedure was employed in the scoring; the rater was unaware of which students were in the experimental group and which were in the control groups. The posttest was given and scored in the same manner 3 months later. In the intervening 3-month time period, the experimental group participated in 12 bibliotherapy-based lessons using the titles selected for literary merit. The control group participated in 12 guidance lessons during the same period of time. Each guidance session was approximately 45 minutes in length. The researcher acted as a leader for both groups.

Instruments

The Paragraph Completion Test was used to measure changes in development associated with conceptual level. *Conceptual level* is defined as a personal characteristic indexing both cognitive complexity and interpersonal maturity (Hunt, 1971). The constructs associated with conceptual level provide a 3-stage sequence directly related to educational objectives. Sprinthall and Sprinthall (1981, pp. 376–377) characterized these stages as follows:

> *Stage 1: Low Conceptual Level.* Generally thinking is concrete and stereotyped. There is a single "right" way to learn. Rules are fixed and unchangeable. Obedience to authority is unquestioned. Problem solving tends to be rigid, and the desire to please others is strong. These children are anxious for closure and seek highly structured learning activities.

Stage 2: Moderate Conceptual Level. Some evidence of tolerance for uncertainty and ambiguity and awareness of alternatives exists, along with some openness to new ideas. There is increased independence in thinking (inner-directedness) and awareness of emotions. Increased inductive inquiry develops.

Stage 3: High Conceptual Level. Evidence appears of integration and synthesis both in complex intellectual and interpersonal arenas. Children weigh and balance alternatives, and can simultaneously process their own views and others. Closure is temporary. The children employ successive approximation and principles in decision making and will not compromise those. They accept full responsibility for consequences of their own behavior.

The Paragraph Completion Test was selected because it had previously been successfully used with upper elementary-early middle school age groups (Cross, 1970; Hunt, Greenwood, Noy, & Watson, 1973). Although developmental theorists recommend the use of two instruments to assess developmental change, we were unable to obtain a second developmental measure that was validated below high school grade levels. The quantitative data gathered were supported, however, through qualitative review of the material available in student journals.

The Paragraph Completion Test evaluates defined conceptual level by providing sentence stems to which individuals are asked to respond with three or four sentences indicating personal reactions. This provides a semi-projective format in areas of conflict, uncertainty, and rule-structured authority relations (Satterstrom, 1980). Construct validity of conceptual level as a personality variable has been summarized by Hunt (1971), Schroder (1971), and Schroder, Driver, and Steufert (1967). Interrater reliabilities for raters with approximately 3 days of training have been established ranging from .80 to .95 (Gardiner & Schroder, 1972). Correlations with intelligence (.09 to .29), age-grade (.08 to .17), social class (middle class higher than lower class), gender (girls higher than boys), academic achievement (.16 to .17), and personality measures (.12 to .34) are also available (Hunt, 1971).

The Intervention

In the experimental group, stories were read aloud and were then followed by counselor-led class discussions and journal writing. Three prompts were used to encourage oral or written response: (a) What did you notice about the story? (b) How did the story make you feel? (c) What does this story remind you of in your own life? These prompts were adapted for counselor use from suggestions by Kelly (1990). Then, using counselor skills of reflection and clarification, issues were allowed to emerge based on student response and need.

The materials for the experimental group were selected not only to meet guidance goals, but also to meet criteria for quality established by experts in the field of children's literature, such as Hearne (1983), Purves and Monson (1984), and Vandergrift (1980). These criteria include evaluation of language, setting, plot, illustrations, characters, and theme. The specific titles for this intervention were selected in consultation with the chair of the Newbery Award Committee, Alice Naylor. Consideration was given to length, adaptability for oral reading, multicultural appeal, and variety of genre. All titles used for this bibliotherapy-based curriculum are additionally indexed in one of two reference books that index titles by theme, but base their listings on quality: *The Bookfinder* (Dreyer, 1985) and *The Children's Catalog* (Isaacson, Hillegas, & Yaakov, 1986).

Final titles selected for the experimental group were *Grandaddy's Place* (Griffith, 1987), *Georgia Music* (Griffith, 1984), *Mufaro's Beautiful Daughters* (Steptoe, 1987), *The Mountains of Tibet* (Gerstein, 1987), *Today was a Terrible Day* (Giff, 1987), *Family Secrets: Five Very Important Stories* (Shreve, 1980), *The Power of Light: Eight Stories for Hanukkah* (Singer, 1980), and *Tuck Everlasting* (Babbitt, 1975). The order of this listing also reflects the sequence of presentation.

Five of the books used were each completed with their discussions in one class period. *Family Secrets* and *The Power of Light* required two class periods each, and *Tuck Everlasting*, three class periods. The two stories used from *Family Secrets* were "The Death of Giles" and "Cheating."

The 12 lessons presented to the control group were selected from story-based guidance curricula designed to teach values and decision making. No attempt was made to apply the criteria for literary excellence. In the first 6 lessons, open-ended dilemmas were read aloud. Children responded with choices of the appropriate behavior and reasons for their choices. Journals, as well as class discussions, were used. Forced choice and rank-order strategies were used to vary the format. In the final 6 lessons, biographical sketches were read aloud that emphasized values such as inventiveness, altruism, friendship, courage, and perseverance. These were followed by oral discussion in large or small groups or journal entries. In all discus-

TABLE 1
A Summary of Pretest–Posttest Mean Scores on the Paragraph Completion Test

Group	n	PCT 1		PCT 2	
		M	SD	M	SD
Control	20	.9425	.2962	1.0595	.4632
Experimental	22	.9559	.3652	1.2509	.3370
Combined	42	.9495	.3302	1.1598	.4086

sions, the leader used reflective statements, encouraging multilevel responses.

Results

The purpose of this research was to evaluate the developmental effects of both a bibliotherapy-based curriculum with selections from quality children's literature and a story-based guidance curriculum that was more didactic in nature. The primary questions addressed were (a) Will the classroom guidance interventions promote developmental growth as measured by the Paragraph Completion Test? (b) Will the curriculum based on quality children's literature be more effective in promoting developmental growth than the traditional guidance curriculum?

An analysis of covariance was used to assess treatment effects. This particular procedure was selected in order to reduce experimental error by statistical means and to adjust treatment effects for any differences between the treatment groups that existed before the start of the intervention (Keppel, 1982). Because pure random assignment of individuals to this study was not possible, the analysis of covariance with pretest scores as the covariate allowed for correction of preexisting differences.

Possible scores on the Paragraph Completion Test (PCT) range from 0 to 3, reflecting associated conceptual levels or stages. On the pretest, the children in both groups (ages 10 and 11) scored slightly under level 1 (control group = .9425; experimental group = .9559). Developmental growth on the PCT was noted in both groups over the 3-month time span (posttest results: control group = 1.0595; experimental group = 1.2509), as can be seen in Table 1.

TABLE 2
An Analysis of Covariance of Intervention Effects

Source	SS	df	MS	F	Sig of F
Covariate	3.308	1	3.308	40.331	—
Main effects	0.339	1	0.339	4.134 *	.049

Note. SS = Sum of squares; MS = mean square.
*$p < .05$.

An analysis of covariance using pretest scores as the covariate was used to secure a more precise estimate of between group differences. The results demonstrate that the developmental growth in the experimental group was greater. Additionally, the between group differences were statistically significant at the .05 alpha level, as noted in Table 2.

Discussion

Additional research will be needed to fully describe the transactions between children and literature and to understand the effects of those transactions on development. Although an initial review of the results of this study is encouraging (related to the use of either of these classroom guidance interventions), there are some limitations that must be acknowledged. The students do not represent a true random sample. Intact classes were used based on principal recommendation. Regardless of efforts to match groups based on teacher style, student ability, and cultural background, much happens in a school classroom and in children's lives during any 3-month period. Isolating a single factor or intervention as being solely responsible for developmental growth would be extremely difficult.

Although these limitations may not be ideal in experimental research, they do reflect the realities of schools, which may be more important. N. L. Gage (1978) in reviewing the prospects related to educational research, noted "Probably none of the generalizations that survive the test of experimentation will permit highly exact prediction or unerring control of educational results. Nonetheless, they will improve substantially on . . . unaided common sense or raw experience . . . " (p. 93). The current study gives us much to consider.

Previous research has indicated that there is no spontaneous growth in developmental stage over a 3- to 6-month period (Rest, 1986) and that conceptual level is stable over the time period involved in the current study (Hunt, 1971). These previous findings suggest very strongly that no change in assessed level of development occurs without carefully designed educative experiences. The conceptual growth in both groups suggests the effectiveness of regular story-based classroom guidance. The results seem particularly encouraging related to the use of quality children's literature. A clearer picture of effectiveness could be obtained with replications of this study, especially if a third group could be added that, during the specified time period, did not receive classroom guidance.

Assessment of the effectiveness of the intervention could also be enhanced by the use of a second instrument. The design or validation of instruments that can be used with younger age groups will be necessary.

Perhaps the most significant contributions of the current study to our "unaided common sense and raw experience" (Gage, 1978) are in challenging our perceptions of bibliotherapeutic approaches and in refining our processes for selecting appropriate materials. Using books in counseling does not have to be reserved for specific situations with individual students, but can also be used as a developmental intervention in classrooms.

Implications

This study has direct implications for school counselors in terms of providing an effective approach for classroom guidance. The use of stories as a method for helping individuals solve problems or better understand themselves appears to have promise not only in motivating therapy (as indicated in previous literature) but also personal growth. The essential components of the more effective intervention in this study were the use of stories of literary merit and the open-ended discussions.

If elementary counselors choose to use bibliotherapeutic approaches in classroom guidance, they may adopt a selective process that begins with bibliographies that index books by theme. The most inclusive of these bibliographies (Dreyer, 1985) addresses the needs and problems of children and youth. Other bibliographies address specific topics such as stress (Gillis, 1978), disabilities (Azarnoff, 1983; Baskin, 1984; Friedberg, 1985), separation and loss (Bernstein, 1983), problems (Hirsch, 1983; Pardeck, 1984), and divorce (Bowker, 1982).

Even in using these resources, the critical issue will continue to be the attention given not only to the topic or theme suggested but also to the literary quality of the selections. Vandergrift (1980), in a critique of thematic bibliographies available to counselor and other professionals, noted that the quality of books selected was rarely considered and that the bibliographies often read like "catalogs of all the world's ills" (p. 282). She warned practitioners against placing children into problem categories simply to match labels on the books, concluding that bibliotherapy at its worst assumes that the book is only about a problem, and at its best is a means of helping a child make connections between books and his or her own life.

Counselors can help children make such connections by selecting stories that affirm their self-worth and offer insights into their relationships with others. In order to identify such stories, counselors may collaborate with media specialists, classroom teachers, parents, and the children themselves. Journals such as *Hornbook* and *The School Library Journal* contain current reviews and supply lists of award-winning books. Some counselors may wish to enroll in a course in children's literature to develop further knowledge of titles and expertise in applying criteria for selection.

Counselors are ideal facilitators for discussions of stories because they have professional skills in active listening, clarification of content, and reflection of feeling. The power of the literary transaction between children and story, coupled with the interaction between a skilled counselor and children, has the potential to become bibliotherapy at its best.

References

American School Counselor Association Position Statements. (1978). *Developmental guidance*. Falls Church, VA: ASCA.

Azarnoff, P. (1983). *Health, illness and disability: A guide to books for children and young adults*. New York: Bowker.

Baruth, L., & Phillips, L. (1976). Bibliotherapy and the school counselor. *The School Counselor, 23*(3), 191–199.

Baskin, B. (1984). *More notes from a different drummer: A guide to juvenile fiction portraying the disabled*. New York: Bowker.

Bernstein, J. (1983). *Books to help children cope with separation and loss* (2nd ed.). New York: Bowker.

Bodart, J. (1980). Bibliotherapy: The right book for the right person at the right time and more. *Top of the News, 36*, 183–188.

Bowker, M. A. (1982). Children and divorce: Being in between. *Elementary School Guidance & Counseling, 17*(2), 126–130.

Coles, R. (1989). *The call of stories: Teaching and the moral imagination.* Boston: Houghton-Mifflin.

Cornett, C. E., & Cornett, C. F. (1980). *Bibliotherapy: The right book at the right time.* Bloomington, IN: Indiana University Press.

Cross, H. J. (1970). The relation of parental training to conceptual structure in pre-adolescents. *Journal of Genetic Psychology, 116,* 197–202.

Dreyer, S. (Ed.). (1985). *The bookfinder: A guide to children's literature about the needs and problems of youth.* Circle Pines, MN: American Guidance Service.

Friedberg, J. (1985). *Accept me as I am: Best books of juvenile nonfiction on impairments and disabilities.* New York: Bowker.

Gage, N. L. (1978). *The scientific basis for the art of teaching.* New York: Teachers College Press.

Gardiner, G. S., & Schroder, H. M. (1972). Reliability and validity of a paragraph completion test: Theoretical and empirical notes. *Psychology Reports, 31,* 959–962.

Gillis, R. J. (1978). *Children's books for times of stress: An annotated bibliography.* Bloomington, IN: Indiana University Press.

Hearne, B. (1983). *Choosing books for children.* New York: Delacorte.

Hirsch, E. (1983). *Problems of early childhood: An annotated bibliography and guide.* New York: Garland.

Hunt, D. E. (1971). *Matching models in education.* Toronto: Ontario Institute for Studies in Education.

Hunt, D. E., Greenwood, J., Noy, J. E., & Watson, H. (1973). *Assessment of CL: Paragraph Completion Method.* Toronto: Ontario Institute for Studies in Education.

Isaacson, R. J., Hillegas, F. E., & Yaakov, J. (Eds.). (1986). *The children's catalog* (15th ed.). New York: H. W. Wilson.

Kelly, P. (1990). Guiding young students' response to literature. *Reading Teacher's Journal, 43*(7), 464–470.

Keppel, G. (1982). *Design and analysis: A researcher's handbook* (2nd ed.). Englewood Cliffs, NJ: Prentice-Hall.

Myrick, R. D. (1987). *Developmental guidance and counseling: A practical approach.* Minneapolis, MN: Educational Media Corporation.

Pardeck, J. J. (1984). *Young people with problems: A guide to bibliotherapy.* New York: Greenwood Press.

Purves, A., & Monson, D. (1984). *Experiencing children's literature.* Glenview, IL: Scott, Foresman and Co.

Rest, J. R. (1986). *Moral development.* New York: Praeger.

Rovenger, J. (1988). Children's literature as a moral compass. *School Library Journal, 33*(8), 45-46.

Satterstrom, L. S. (1980). A matching model for differentiated supervision of student teachers. Unpublished doctoral dissertation, University of Minnesota. *Dissertation Abstracts International, 41*, 3062A.
Schrank, F. A. (1982). Bibliotherapy as an elementary guidance tool. *Elementary School Guidance & Counseling, 16*(3), 218–227.
Schroder, H. M. (1971). Conceptual complexity and personality organization. In H. M. Schroder & P. Snefeld (Eds.), *Personality theory and information processing*. New York: Ronald Press.
Schroder, H. M., Driver, M. J., & Streufert, S. (1967). *Human information processing*. New York: Holt, Rinehart & Winston.
Sprinthall, N. A., & Sprinthall, W. A. (1981). *Educational psychology: A developmental approach*. Reading, MA: Addison-Wesley.
Vandergrift, K. (1980). *Child and story: The literary connection*. New York: Neal-Schuman.

Additional Resources

The following stories were used with the experimental group in the study.

Babbit, N. (1975). *Tuck everlasting*. New York: Farrar, Straus, Giroux.
Gerstein, M. (1987). *The mountains of Tibet*. New York: Harper.
Giff, P. (1987). *Today was a terrible day*. Melrose Park, IL: Puffin.
Griffith, H. (1987). *Grandaddy's place*. New York: Greenwillow.
Griffith, H. (1984). *Georgia music*. New York: Greenwillow.
Shreve, S. (1980). *Family secrets: Five very important stories*. New York: Dell Yearling Books.
Singer, I. (1980). *The power of light: Eight stories for Hanukkah*. New York: Farrar, Straus, Giroux.
Steptoe, J. (1987). *Mufaro's beautiful daughers*. New York: Lothrop.

An additional helpful resource is the following:

Borders, S., & Naylor, A. (1993). *Talking with children about books*. Phoenix, AZ: Oryx Press.

CHAPTER 7

Peer Counseling for Middle School Students Experiencing Family Divorce: A Deliberate Psychological Education Model

Norman A. Sprinthall, Janice S. Hall, and Edwin R. Gerler, Jr.

As family life in the final decade of the 1900s becomes more complex through disruptions such as divorce, single-parent families, and blended families, there is an inevitable pressure on school counseling services to respond constructively to such difficulties. At the same time, due to either budget cuts or rapid expansion of student populations, professional school counselors often find themselves confronted with genuine resource allocation dilemmas. Almost any counselor would immediately ask, "How can I provide enough services either for individuals or small groups when my own schedule is already jammed with testing, advising, working with parents, teachers, class schedule changes, and the like?" Admittedly this is not an entirely new prob-

---

This chapter is taken directly from Sprinthall, N. A., Hall, J. S., & Gerler, E. R. (1992). Peer counseling for middle school students experiencing family divorce: A deliberate psychological education model. *Elementary School Guidance and Counseling, 26*(4), 279–294.

lem (Mathewson, 1949); yet, with a continued increase in family disruptions through divorce there has been an increased need for such psychological services (Baruth & Burggraf, 1983; Bundy & Gumaer, 1984). In fact, Hetherington's (1984) extensive research has documented the range of problems and difficulties created by parental divorce, separation, or both. Most recently she has found clear evidence that the time of greatest vulnerability is during early adolescence. Her research showed that well over half of young teenagers reacted to divorce with psychological upset so extensive as to seem pathological (Hetherington, 1989). Ironically, other recent research (Ursone, 1990) has shown that such children do not seek out school counseling services because of the perception that school counselors are already too busy with other tasks.

Peer Counseling: An Untapped Resource

Although the concept of peer counseling had been researched a number of years ago (Mosher & Sprinthall, 1971) and there is a national network organization—The National Peer Helper Association—designed to promote the concept, at best the idea remains on the fringe of school programs. None of the recent spate of school reform proposals mentions anything about the potency of such a model for providing needed psychological assistance to students during difficult transition periods (Adler, 1983; Boyer, 1983; Sizer, 1984). As a result of the need to provide services for psychological help during a major disruption, and to demonstrate once again the effectiveness of a peer model, the current study was designed. High school students became peer counselors for groups of middle school students experiencing a family divorce.

Directing Constructs

The theoretical orientation for the study was based on cognitive developmental concepts, particularly Loevinger's (1976) theory of stages of ego development. Briefly, her theory suggests that ego- or self-awareness may proceed in a stage and sequence framework through levels of psychological differentiation and integration. Recent longitudinal research has shown that adolescents under appropriate circumstances of positive interaction will proceed from self-protective ego levels to a level of social conformity (Gfellner, 1986) during the middle school to high school time periods. Other research (Loevinger, 1979) has shown that higher stages of ego development are more adaptive and can result in more comprehensive and effective personal problem solving.

A second theoretical question concerns the framework for psychological development. Loevinger's work has supported the rationale for selecting ego stage theory. Her work, however, does not focus on the educational or instructional question. In fact, she is ambivalent over the prospect of school programs designed with such developmental stage growth goals (Loevinger, 1976, p. 453). It was the original work of Kohlberg (1975) and Selman (1971) that provided part of the theoretical basis for the educational program in the current study. They suggested, from George Herbert Mead's (1934) contention, that actual role-taking experiences could produce the conditions for developmental growth. Although Loevinger's work suggested that developmental stage predicts certain human behaviors (i.e., stage as an independent variable), the Kohlberg and Selman work suggested that developmental stage became the dependent variable (i.e., the target of educational interventions). This meant that role-taking programs could be designed to enhance the developmental stage of the participants. Two recent studies (Kessler, Ibrahim, & Kahn, 1986; Sprinthall & Scott, 1989) have supported that contention.

An additional reason for the role-taking approach as an intervention method concerns the question of format or types of experience. Dewey (1944) pointed out that not all experiences are necessarily educative. It is certainly easy to think of role-taking experiences that would be miseducative, psychonoxious, and growth retarding (e.g., teaching teenagers how to become drug dealers or drug users). It was based on this question that we selected a form of peer counseling as an appropriate role-taking experience. Earlier research, as noted, had shown that such experiences in role-taking, learning effective helping skills and including, "the iron discipline of listening" (L. Kohlberg, personal communication, 1971) helped promote stage growth. Thus it seemed if we wished to promote more complex cognitive structures for adolescents, peer counseling would be most appropriate. In selecting helping experience as the objective of the role-taking intervention, we focused on the counseling skills necessary to become effective in that role. Two recent massive meta-analyses (Eisenberg & Miller, 1987; Miller & Eisenberg, 1988) have shown consistently positive relationships between empathy and prosocial human behavior on one hand and a negative relationship between the lack of empathy and aggressive or antisocial behavior on the other hand. Thus the role-taking experiences were selected as appropriately educative and designed to enhance ego stage growth through intensive empathy training.

A final theoretical reason for the approach concerns the so-called "plus one" question (Rest, 1973; Turiel, 1966). Although it has usually been cast in intellectual terms (i.e., an understanding and appreciation of thinking at a slightly more complex stage), the idea can also be attributed to personal modeling (Bandura, 1977). It was our view that training a group of high school students as peer helpers provided middle school students with slightly older peers as plus one models. Generally, as a result of the strict age segregation of most public schools, the early adolescents themselves rarely come into contact—let alone positive contact—with senior high students. We also thought that such cross-age relationships would help to reinforce the ideas of responsibility and maturity by the high school students. In a sense the interpersonal plus one idea is interactive; the early adolescents might respond positively to their older models and the models themselves may become more mature from the responsibility.

Research Design

Experimental Groups

The students for the study were in two intact elective classes at a large suburban high school. Students from the 11th and 12th grades had been recommended for enrollment by teachers, counselors, and students on the basis of their maturity and ability to relate to others. A total of 28 had chosen to be physical education aides, and 24 had chosen to be peer counselors. The physical education aides were chosen as a control group. Although that group had a curriculum that included the development of communication skills, it did not provide for as much in-depth training or guided reflection as was the case with the two experimental programs.

The 24 students in the peer counselor group were chosen as the experimental groups. Of the 24, 10 would colead groups of students from divorced families and were designated as Experimental Group I. The other 14 would colead groups of students from a variety of other school settings and were designated as Experimental Group II.

The middle school students experiencing a family disruption were identified by the counselors from two middle schools. They created five groups of eight pupils each for the focus on family disruptions. The other groups for the second experimental group were formed to focus on representative problems of elementary and middle school students such as self-esteem, achievement, and social isolation.

Measures

The high school peer counselors in the two experimental groups and one control group were assessed on a pretest–posttest basis with the 18-item version of the Loevinger Sentence Completion Test (Loevinger, Wessler, & Redmore, 1970) as the main dependent variable. We used the shortened multiple measurement on a pretest–posttest basis. The high school students were also assessed on the same basis with the Rest Defining Issues Test (Rest, 1986). The former measures stages of ego development; the latter measures levels of principled reasoning. Both measures have substantial and established reliability and validity.

The middle school students were assessed on a pretest–posttest basis with the 18-item Loevinger and the Nowicki–Strickland Locus of Control Scale (Nowicki & Strickland, 1973). (Like the Loevinger, the Nowicki–Strickland measure has well-established reliability and validity.) We were not able to create a comparison group for the middle school students in the divorce-disruption group. In order to have sufficient numbers of high school students in the first experimental group, we needed to take all of the identified middle school students ($N = 40$) to form five groups to be co-led by the 10 high school students. A second consideration was the realization that many of the groups in the second experimental condition comprehended such a wide variety of issues that it would prevent any generalization. Although the lack of a contemporaneous control for the middle school group does threaten the validity of outcome, it should also be noted that both the Loevinger and the Nowicki–Strickland measures do not ordinarily show change from maturity over the time period of the current study.

The Educational Intervention

Overview. The experimental program was designed to meet the guidelines for educational programs that focus on the psychological development of the participants. In addition to a significant role-taking experience, the program included systematic reflection, continuity for at least one semester, and a balance between role-taking and reflection. This model is really quite similar to graduate professional programs that meld academic seminars with guided application through practica (Sprinthall & Thies-Sprinthall, 1983). By combining the experiential with the reflective, broader educative goals can be achieved.

Peer Counseling Training Program for High School Students. The training program for the high school students involved a 1-semester course in peer helping. The content of the training varied in accordance with the targeted intervention. The program for all groups involved traditional peer counselor skill training and practice with content from *An In-Depth Look at Training Peer Helpers* (Tindall & Gray, 1985) and similar material. For the divorce group leaders there was also focused material from *The Changing Family* (Ciborowski, 1984) as well as some video material from other sources highlighting the issues involved. The curriculum guide for training the divorce group leaders can be found in Appendix A. The peer counselor training classes were co-led by a counselor and a teacher. The high school students enrolled in these training classes kept weekly journals for reflection on the process. The coleaders had substantial prior experience in peer counselor training.

Role-Taking Experiences of the High School Students. During the second semester the high school students in the experimental groups met with their middle school students twice each week for discussions. The high school students also met with the peer training instructors each week for reflection, discussion, and planning. The divorce group leaders ($N = 10$) met with the counselor and the regular peer counseling leaders ($N = 14$) met with the teacher. Both groups of leaders continued to keep journals that were turned in weekly for comment by the teacher or the counselor. The control group high school students engaged in helping activities through physical education instruction. They did not keep journals or meet for reflective discussions.

Results

The major statistical analysis for the high school student leaders was a one-way analysis of variance (ANOVA) across the three groups, two experimental and one control. Table 1 presents the results.

TABLE 1
ANOVA Results for Three Groups of High School Students on the Loevinger and Rest Measures of Development

Group	Pretest M	Pretest SD	Posttest M	Posttest SD	Gain Score	F
Loevinger Sentence Completion Test						
Experimental 1 (n = 10)	5.90	1.37	6.70	1.31	0.80	6.63
Experimental 2 (n = 14)	6.07	1.07	6.43	1.15	0.36	(p<.05)
Control (n = 24)	5.79	1.25	5.58	1.19	−0.21	
Rest Defining Issues Test Principled Scores						
Experimental 1 (n = 10)	25.66	12.06	33.35	12.01	7.69	0.91
Experimental 2 (n = 14)	29.99	12.20	29.77	12.15	−0.22	(ns)
Control (n = 14)	21.11	12.35	22.35	12.29	1.24	

Note. The Loevinger stages were transformed to integers in accordance with her recommendations (Loevinger, 1976, p. 240). In this case stage 2 = 1, Δ = 2, Δ3 = 3, 3 = 4, 3/4 = 5, 4 = 6, and 4/5 = 7.

Statistical Analysis

Results for the High School Students on the Loevinger Instrument. The Loevinger protocols were scored by a workshop-trained rater. The interjudge reliability of her ratings was established at +.91. The results indicated that there was a statistically significant difference across the three groups. To determine the relative contribution by group, the Fisher PLSD (Winer, 1971) was employed. Those results showed that the gain scores for both experimental groups were significantly different from the control. The divorce group leaders gained almost a full stage on the Loevinger from just below I (Integrative) level Four toward I level Four-Five. The peer counseling group also improved from I level Four halfway to I level Four-Five. The control group remained essentially stable just below I level Four with a slight posttest decline. Such a decline is apparently expected as a result of a variety of testing factors, according to Redmore and Waldman (1979).

Results for the High School Students on the Rest Instrument. The results from the Rest Defining Issues Test are also presented in Table 1. The results indicate that on an overall basis the gain scores were not statistically significant. Inspection of the mean pretest–posttest scores shows that the second experimental group and the control group remained the same. The first experimental group showed a positive trend from a Principled (P) score of 25.66 to 33.35, a gain of almost 8

TABLE 2
Analysis of Gain Scores for Middle School Students on the Loevinger and the Nowicki–Strickland Measures

Measure	n	M	SD	Gain Score	Paired t (one-tail)
Loevinger Sentence Completion Test					
Pretest	40	4.20	1.24	0.35	3.00 ($p < .002$)
Posttest	40	4.55	1.36		
Nowicki–Strickland Locus of Control Scale					
Pretest	40	15.55	4.06	−2.27	3.27 ($p < .001$)
Posttest	40	13.28	3.92		

Note. The same conversion to integers was used for middle school students on the Loevinger stage scores (see Table 1 Note).

points. Rest (1986) has shown that gain scores usually need to exceed the standard error of measurement of 9 points to reach significance. From this we may conclude a positive trend in favor of the first experimental group rather than significance beyond the .05 level. The other groups showed no such trends.

Results for the Middle School Students. The results for the middle school students are presented in Table 2. Because there was no control group, the Direct Difference Method (Sprinthall, 1990) was employed to test significance. In this method a higher level of statistical difference is required through dividing the degrees of freedom in half to offset the likelihood of a Type I error. Table 2 indicates that the .35 gain from Delta Three toward I level Three was significant on the Loevinger. Table 2 also indicates that a negative gain of 2.27 on the Nowicki–Strickland was also significant. A lower score on this measure indicates an increase in personal efficacy and control.

Summary of Empirical Results. Taken as a whole, these empirical results support the developmental goals of the program for both the high school students and the middle school students. The former made significant gains on the stage of ego development toward stage Four-Five. Characteristics of self-awareness and problem solving at that level include an increase in interpersonal awareness, greater understanding of the complexities and paradoxes of life, psychological causation, individuality, and the gradual internalization of standards for mature judgment.

For the middle school students the development was away from self-protectiveness and seeing obedience and conformity as absolutes and toward some individuality, a rudimentary inner life psychologically, and a greater awareness of self in relationships to others. Also the increase in locus of control toward the self and away from other-directedness complemented the change in ego stage level.

Qualitative Results

In addition to the empirical data, we also collected excerpts from some of the student journals to add some subjective or qualitative information about the program effects. These excerpts can be found in Appendix B, and they illustrate some important themes. The high school students tended to focus their discussions, especially in the training sessions, on themselves and some of their own personal agendas. By the second semester there was some broadening of perspective taking and more willingness to think and feel about what the middle school students were experiencing. The excerpts from the middle school students reveal their positive feelings about the process and some commentary about an increase in self-awareness. These themes tend to confirm the changes documented through the empirical measures.

Discussion

The study can be considered as demonstrating the positive interactive effects of peer counseling. Under appropriate conditions both the peer helpers and their students benefit from the experience. In the former case Skovholt (1974) termed this "the helper principle." This indicates that placing a high school student in a responsible role is not exploitative. Indeed, the opposite is true. The principle is based on findings similar to those of this study, namely that the helper becomes more psychologically mature, exhibits greater self-awareness, and improves in perspective-taking capacity. The role-taking experience, as Kohlberg (1975) noted, provides a means of promoting stage cognitive-developmental growth. It is also important to note the lack of effects in the control group. These students participated in a continuous helping experience of the same duration. They had also volunteered and been recommended by the school staff. The results, however, indicated no change on either developmental measure. This would confirm Dewey's (1944) contention that experience alone may or may not enhance growth. The control group students did not have the opportunity to discuss or reflect upon their leadership role. There was no seminar for guided examination. In a sense then, the control group experience of what is sometimes called service or experiential learning could verge on exploitation. It certainly raises an important consideration concerning any proposals for national service learning programs at the high school or college level.

A second issue is the changed role for school professionals, namely teachers and counselors, and in particular the latter. We noted at the outset of this article the continuing time dilemma faced by school counselors: too many students, too many needs, and too many demands. By changing the role from direct service provider to that of consultant or resource teacher, school personnel, particularly counselors, may increase their effectiveness. Certainly it was clear in the current study that both the teacher-counselor team and the high school students ended up with vastly different conceptions of each other. The adults were extremely impressed by the resourcefulness, the insight, and the responsibility exhibited by the high school helpers. The students themselves often commented how different the peer training class was compared to conventional courses. They saw the adults as genuine resource educators who not only helped them with the skills but also were responsive to them on a personal level. The authority of the adults was not challenged but rather was seen more as the authority inherent in older colleagues. The atmosphere in the training classes resembled a community of helpers, which the students very much appreciated. Although we had no formal measure of atmosphere, on a subjective basis we thought that such a climate was an important contributor to positive outcomes, certainly necessary but not sufficient by itself.

A third issue of significance, specifically for the first experimental group, concerns the sensitive issue of family divorce. We had worried a great deal about these questions from both perspectives. Would the high school students really understand the personal complexities involved and be able to provide the necessary support to encourage clarification and discussions? Also, how would the middle school students react to the opportunity to discuss such personal concerns, particularly in view of Hetherington's (1989) findings of behavior verging on the pathological? We also knew that the Ursone study (1990) in progress at the time had shown, retrospectively, a reluctance on the part of teenagers to discuss such issues with school counselors. Also, we were unsure of possible parental anxieties even though each parent had been contacted and approved of the participation. As a result of such a large number of unknowns, we decided to err on the side of conservatism and included a counselor as an observer for the early sessions. This proved to be unnecessary as it became obvious that the training and continuous seminar meetings provided the leaders with both support and skills to manage the groups very well from a process standpoint. Moreover, after the initial period of group formation, the middle school students were appropriately disclosing of their concerns. In reviewing the sessions, we realized that one of the real and perhaps hidden agenda benefits of the small group method was the opportunity to find out that other peers were experiencing many of the same issues surrounding divorce. Harry Stack Sullivan (1947) years ago maintained, in somewhat ironic language, that early adolescents need to outgrow "the delusion of uniqueness." Another way to put it would be David Elkind's (1967) concept of an excessive egocentrism that accompanies the onset of adolescence. The program seemed to provide a welcomed opportunity to reflect upon such concerns of the early adolescents and to improve their ability to see themselves and the changing family environment in greater perspective.

The final issue concerns the larger question of the school context, particularly the need to reconsider such role-taking programs. The program described here was similar in general outcomes to another contemporaneous study in which high school students (in that case female students) were involved in role taking as cross-age math tutors to fifth-grade girls (Sprinthall & Scott, 1989). The results were also similar, with the high school girls improving on indexes of psychological maturity and the fifth graders improving on their ability to attribute school sucess to themselves and to improve their actual academic achievement in math. These current studies, then, are reminders of the positive effects of providing high school students with carefully sequenced and guided role-taking experiences. It is unfortunate indeed that the requisite school reform proposals continue to overlook the most obvious and potent resources for changing the deadly rote-passive-worksheet routines of most high schools (Goodlad, 1984; Leonard, 1983; Sedlack, Wheeler, Pullin, & Cusick, 1986). In fact, it is noteworthy as well as depressing to review such studies concerning the context in secondary schools and to see how little has changed. Years ago Friedenberg (1959) warned educators that a continuation of the passivity of the hidden curriculum at the secondary level would literally cause adolescents to vanish. There is little evidence that current schooling has heeded that warning.

On a more positive note, Konopka (1973) underlined the importance of development. She commented: "Adolescents are persons with specific qualities and characteristics who have a participatory and responsible role to play, tasks to perform, skills to develop at that particular time" (p. 316). Perhaps during the coming decade school programs will provide such an opportunity for growth; otherwise the current context of schooling may only reinforce a diminishing role for adolescents.

References

Adler, M. (1983). *Paideia problems and possibilities*. New York: Macmillan.
Bandura, A. (1977). *Social learning theory*. Englewood Cliffs, NJ: Prentice-Hall.
Baruth, L., & Burggraf, M. (1983). Helping single-parent families. *Counseling and Human Development, 15*, 1–15.
Boyer, E. (1983). *High school: A report on secondary education in America*. New York: Harper & Row.
Bundy, M., & Gumaer, J. (1984). Families in transition. *Elementary School Guidance & Counseling, 19*, 4–8.
Ciborowski, P. (1984). *The changing family*. Port Chester, NY: Stratman Educational Systems.
Dewey, J. (1944). *Democracy and education*. New York: The Free Press.
Eisenberg, N., & Miller, P. (1987). The relation of empathy to prosocial and related behaviors. *Psychological Bulletin, 101*, 91–119.
Elkind, D. (1967). Egocentrism in adolescence. *Child Development, 38*, 1025–1038.
Friedenberg, E. Z. (1959). *The vanishing adolescent*. Boston: Beacon.
Gfellner, B. (1986). Changes in ego and moral development in adolescents. *Journal of Adolescence, 9*, 281–302.
Goodlad, J. (1984). *A place called school*. New York: McGraw-Hill.
Hetherington, E. M. (1984). Families in transition: The processes of dissolution and reconstruction. In R. Parke (Ed.), *Review of child development research* (pp. 398–440). Chicago: University of Chicago Press.
Hetherington, E. M. (1989, March). *The impact of divorce on families: Current research*. Paper presented at the Society for Research on Adolescence, Atlanta, Georgia.
Kessler, G., Ibrahim, A., & Kahn, H. (1986). Character development in adolescents. *Adolescence, 21*, 109.
Kohlberg, L. (1975). Counseling and counselor education: A developmental approach. *Counselor Education and Supervision, 14*, 250–256.

Konopka, G. (1973). Requirements for healthy development of adolescent youth. *Adolescence, 31,* 291–316.

Leonard, G. (1983). Car pool: A story of public education in the eighties. *Esquire, 99,* 62.

Loevinger, J. (1976). *Ego development.* San Francisco: Jossey-Bass.

Loevinger, J. (1979). Construct validity of the sentence completion test of ego development. *Applied Psychological Measurement, 3,* 281–311.

Loevinger, J., Wessler, R., & Redmore, C. (1970). *Measuring ego development II: Scoring manual for women and girls.* San Francisco: Jossey-Bass.

Mathewson, R. (1949). *Guidance policy and practice.* New York: Harper.

Mead, G. H. (1934). *Mind, self, and society.* Chicago: University of Chicago Press.

Miller, P., & Eisenberg, N. (1988). The relation of empathy to aggressive and externalizing/antisocial behavior. *Psychological Bulletin, 103,* 324–344.

Mosher, R., & Sprinthall, N. (1971). Psychological education in secondary schools: A program to promote individual and human development. *American Psychologist, 25,* 911–924.

Nowicki, S., & Strickland, B. (1973). A locus of control scale for children. *Journal of Consulting and Clinical Psychology, 40,* 148–154.

Redmore, C., & Waldman, K. (1979). Reliability of a sentence completion measure of ego development. *Journal of Personality Assessment, 39,* 239–243.

Rest, J. R. (1973). Patterns of preference and comprehension in moral judgment. *Journal of Personality, 41,* 86–109.

Rest, J. R. (1986). *Moral development.* New York: Praeger.

Sedlack, M., Wheeler, C., Pullin, O., & Cusick, P. (1986). *Selling students short.* New York: Teachers College Press.

Selman, R. E. (1971). The relation of role-taking to the development of moral judgment in children. *Child Development, 42,* 79–91.

Sizer, R. (1984). *Horace's compromise.* Boston: Houghton-Mifflin.

Skovholt, T. (1974). The client as helper: A measure to promote psychological growth. *The Counseling Psychologist, 4,* 58–64.

Sprinthall, N., & Thies-Sprinthall, L. (1983). The teacher as an adult learner: A cognitive-developmental view. In G. Griffin (Ed.), *Staff development* (pp. 13–35). Chicago: National Society for the Study of Education.

Sprinthall, N. A., & Scott, J. (1989). Promoting psychological development, math achievement, and success attribution of female students through deliberate psychological education. *Journal of Counseling Psychology, 36,* 440–446.

Sprinthall, R.C. (1990). *Basic statistical analysis.* Englewood Cliffs, NJ: Prentice-Hall.

Sullivan, H. S. (1947). *Conceptions of modern psychiatry.* Washington, DC: William Alanson White Psychiatric Foundation.

Tindall, J., & Gray, H. (1985). *Becoming an effective peer helper: Book 1. Introductory program* (2nd ed.). Muncie, IN: Accelerated Development.

Turiel, E. (1966). An experimental test of the sequentiality of developmental stages in the child's moral judgment. *Journal of Personality and Social Psychology, 3,* 611–618.

Ursone, D. (1990). *Parental divorce during childhood: In-school programming, outside-of-school support, and effects on perceived social relationships of young adults.* Unpublished master's thesis, North Carolina State University, Raleigh.

Winer, B. J. (1971). *Statistical principles in experimental design.* New York: McGraw-Hill.

APPENDIX A

Peer Counseling Training Curriculum for High School Students

First-Semester Course Content for High School Students:

I. Awareness and appreciation of self and others in the group (4 weeks)
   A. Journal keeping
   B. Value and belief system
   C. Exercise patterns-relaxation
   D. Dietary habits
   E. Interpersonal relationships
   F. Self-esteem
   G. Reach course
   H. Plan and conduct newcomers' groups

II. Helping skills (4 weeks)
   A. Helper attitudes and values
   B. Establishing a helping relationship
      1. Empathy
      2. Nonverbal behavior
      3. Door openers
   C. Ways of listening and responding
      1. Paraphrasing
      2. Summarizing
      3. Clarifying
      4. Reflecting feelings
      5. Nondirective leading
   D. Feedback
   E. Confronting skills
   F. Decision-making skills

III. Grief and loss (3 weeks)
   A. Recognizing change and loss as part of life
   B. Understanding grief
   C. Death and dying
      1. Personal perspectives
      2. Cultural perspectives and customs
      3. Death by self-destruction: suicide
      4. Care settings for the dying
   D. Helping yourself . . . helping others through grief
   E. Community resources for loss and grief
   F. The art of grieving: healing and growing through change

IV. Group facilitation skills (4 weeks)
   A. Groups and group behavior
      1. Definition of a group
      2. Theory of group development
      3. Membership issues in a group
      4. Group norms
      5. Group versus individual goals
      6. Leadership styles and behaviors
   B. Group leadership
      1. Establishing ground rules
      2. Setting group goals
      3. Energizing a group
      4. Designing structured group activities
      5. Conducting a group discussion
      6. Conducting a group process
      7. Diagnosing group problems
      8. Handling problem behaviors
      9. Closure
     10. Evaluation
   C. Understanding early adolescence
      1. Physical
      2. Emotional

V. Understanding effect of disrupted families on teenagers (2 weeks)
   A. Psychological tasks of children of divorce
   B. Coping with family changes
      1. Redefining the family
      2. Single-parent families
      3. Stepparents and blended families
   C. How teenagers survive divorce
      1. The first year
      2. The long run

VI. Making lesson plans (1 week)

Second-Semester Course Content for High School Students (Typical second-semester week of training activities):

  Monday: Planning seminar led by classroom teacher for all 24 students in Experimental Groups I and II.
  Tuesday: Peer leaders colead groups at middle school.
  Wednesday: Peer leaders in Experimental Group I meet with coun-

selor for guided reflection. Peer leaders in Experimental Group II lead middle school group.

Thursday: Peer leaders colead middle school groups.

Friday: Guided reflection led by classroom teacher for all 24 students in Experimental Groups I and II.

APPENDIX B

Journal Excerpts for High School and Middle School Students

High School Student Entries: Student 1

November Entry: I really like coleading the group of new high school students today—good practice for next semester. Mostly I just feel good and comfortable about this class. I feel closer to the students in here than to anybody else at school. But _____, I would like to talk to you about my dad at lunch tomorrow about _____, okay?

April Entry: I'm glad we meet together at least once a week in here, but it sure feels different from when we met every day.

We tried your suggestion about changing everybody's seat yesterday. It helped some with more kids talking. They liked the "talking to an empty chair" lesson a lot! _____ and _____ really got angry talking to their pretend stepsisters but when the group discussed what happened they looked okay with it. _____ didn't seem to like anything but the pizza, but we've got 4 more weeks. Maybe he'll lighten up. I want to talk to you after class about his pain.

Student 2
December Entry: This grief and loss stuff is almost too heavy. Here's the poem I want you to read to the class:

COMES THE DAWN
After a while you learn the subtle difference
Between holding a hand and chaining a soul,
And you learn that love doesn't mean security,
And you begin to learn that kisses aren't contracts
And presents aren't promises
And you begin to accept your defeats
With your head up and your eyes open,
With the grace of a woman, not the grief of a child,
And you learn to build all your roads
On today because tomorrow's ground is too uncertain,
And futures have
A way of falling down in midflight,
After a while you learn that even sunshine burns if you get too much.
So you plant your own garden and decorate your own soul, instead of
  waiting

And you learn that you really can endure . . .
That you really are strong,
And you really do have worth
And you learn and learn
With every goodbye you learn.

May Entry: I can't believe how _____ and _____ are so upbeat in the group when I know how bad it is for them without their dads even living in this town. It does seem like the group really helps and just being friends of each other helps. _____ wrote in her journal that she is glad just to see _____ and me on Tuesdays to see how we look. But _____ and I know there's more going on, lots more.

Student 3

October Entry: I trust some people in the group but not all of them. Hope you don't mind if I don't have much to say about what I think right now.

May Entry: Today _____ and I led the group off the subject (as usual) and talked about risks. They really liked it and opened up so that I think the level of trust is much better. I share a simple risk with them but this is the one I thought about—what happened with me and my car . . . I had it out one day, minding my own business and was driving with traffic. Everyone knew about this car that lived in town. Then, this old Camaro, of course, he wanted to race, shot out in front of me and I went after him. I was going at least 80 mph to 90 mph in the rain having some fun, I thought. When I got a hold on myself, I slowed down and was lucky I didn't get a ticket. I won by the way, I was ashamed and didn't prove a thing.

The kids in the group had a lot of show-off risks to tell about but I did not know if it was "appropriate"—your word—to share mine. What do you think?

Student 4

September Entry: Yes, communication skills are what it's all about. My family communicates with each other well but I don't know if we communicate well with other people.

March Entry: Seems like I communicate better with these middle school kids than with some of my high school friends. My family doesn't have much in common with these kids' families but I think I do . . .

Yesterday we were talking in Psychology about religion. It got really involved. I don't usually come out and talk about my religion since

I'm a Mormon. A lot of people have a lot of harsh views towards Mormons, so I never really talk about my religion unless I know the person real well. After class yesterday I went up to my teacher and asked him what he thought about Mormons. To me that was scary. He seemed to know a lot about religion though, and I wanted to know his views on Mormonism. We had a nice talk. He wasn't hostile at all. I really enjoyed the talk. It helped me to overcome a little fear I had of telling people what I believe. I'm not ashamed of my religion, but I was afraid of the way some people react when I tell them I'm a Mormon.

Student 5
October Entry: Why am I in this class? You wonder why I don't talk probably. I'm scared I'll look and sound silly. I like kids but if that's the only reason I'm here, that's not enough. I'm so different from the rest of these kids.

March Entry: Today, two things were better. First, I took leadership of the group—not _____. We did that "Common Feelings About Divorce" lesson and discussed guilty, sad, angry, disappointed. Mostly the kids talked, but I knew I kept it directed.

Middle School Student Entries: Student 1

What I really enjoyed about this class was when _____ and _____ could always give good advice anytime you need it. And they always seem to be there when you need them. I hate to see them go because they're really special even if _____ always likes to say "chill-out." But it never bothered me. There is nothing I never liked about this class. I think this class has really helped me out mentally. It made me realize what me and my family really is and can be. I hope when I join this class next year they'll be the leaders.
Student 2
Liked talking about what I did on weekends. Kool getting drinks and things.
Student 3
I already am helping my family get better by understanding and listening. I am close to my stepmother.
Student 4
The most important reason I see in marrying is to live in happiness and not be lonely.
Student 5
I am learning to work on my troubles when things come up.

Student 6
I really liked this group. It was fun, and I felt free to talk about things, and I learned how other people feel about divorced parents and what they did in problem situations.

Student 7
I like this group because it helps me with family problems and is relaxing. I would like to lead a group like this when I'm a junior in high school—with somebody else.

CHAPTER 8

The Dilemma in Drug Abuse Prevention

Robert Paisley, Edwin R. Gerler, Jr., and Norman A. Sprinthall

Why do adolescents abuse alcohol and other drugs? Many counselors answer that peer pressure is the major factor. Carter (1983), for one, stated that "teenagers most strongly influence each other regarding dress and appearance, choice of leisure-time activities, language, and use of alcohol and drugs" (p. 25). Although efforts to reduce this pressure to use drugs have usually not succeeded, some prevention programs have shown promise. Horan and Williams's (1982) study of an assertiveness training program designed to help adolescents resist pressure to use drugs showed that junior high school students who participated in the training were significantly less inclined toward drug abuse than were students who did not participate. Similarly, the "Skills for Adolescence" curriculum developed by the Quest National Center in Columbus, Ohio, has shown promise in helping adolescents to deal effectively with peer pressure and to consider positive alternatives to drug use (Gerler, 1986). These programs are interesting because they depart from past drug education efforts that concentrated on provid-

---

This chapter is taken directly from Paisley, R.T., Gerler, E.R., & Sprinthall, N.A. (1990). The dilemma in drug abuse prevention. *The School Counselor*, *38*(2), 113–122.

ing students with drug information and neglected the interpersonal and emotional factors involved in substance abuse among adolescents.

It is becoming evident, however, that even the current promising approaches to drug abuse prevention do not focus sufficiently on how adolescents reason when confronted with peer pressure to use drugs. The need to correct this deficiency in drug education programs is particularly apparent from a recent study (Mohr, Sprinthall, & Gerler, 1987) that showed that early adolescents tend to use lower levels of moral judgment when confronted with drug-related dilemmas than when faced with other kinds of dilemmas. This finding suggests that decisions about drug use are especially troublesome to adolescents and, therefore, that counselors need to find ways for increasing the level of adolescents' reasoning about drug-related dilemmas.

Progress in cognitive development theory and research offer the hope that innovative programs may be developed to advance the level of reasoning adolescents use when confronted with pressure to use drugs and, in turn, result in adolescents becoming more individuated and less influenced by peers who decide to experiment with drugs. Loevinger's (1977) work in the area of ego development, Kohlberg's (1979) work in moral development, and Selman's (1980) study of children's abilities to process complex interpersonal situations have led to the development of innovative group discussion techniques focused on students' reasoning about social and psychological dilemmas. These discussion techniques challenge students' reasoning about common social dilemmas faced during adolescence and provide students with role-taking experiences to gain insight into the thinking of peers. This study examines the application of these discussion techniques to drug abuse prevention with the aim of advancing the level of thinking adolescents use when facing the dilemma of whether or not to use drugs. This study examines the following question: Will a short-term, drug abuse prevention curriculum that challenges students' thinking about drug use through discussion and reflection on drug-related dilemmas promote the process of individuation among adolescents by advancing students' moral reasoning and increasing their conceptual level?

Method

Participants

The 52 students involved in this study were ninth graders enrolled in health classes at a large suburban high school in North Carolina. The participants included 28 girls and 24 boys from varying economic, social, and cultural environments. The drug educator involved in the study was a doctoral-level counselor who had extensive leadership experience with groups of adolescents.

Procedure

Enrollment in the ninth grade health classes used for this study was determined by computerized random selection carried out by school officials. For research purposes students from these classes were then randomly assigned to experimental and control groups. Experimental group 1 consisted of nine girls and five boys. Experimental group 2 was made up of six girls and eight boys. The remaining students (13 girls and 11 boys) served as controls.

The Drug Abuse Prevention Program. Participants in the two experimental groups received identical treatments. They took part in 12 one-hour, small group sessions, which were conducted on consecutive days. A pretest-introduction session preceded implementation of the program and a posttest-exit session followed it. Students kept personal journals of thoughts and feelings about each group session and could volunteer to discuss their journal entries at the beginning of each session.

Session 1. Group members paired off, separated from the group for approximately 5 minutes, and got acquainted with each other. Members returned to the group and introduced each other to the entire group. The leader then discussed the goals of dilemma discussion groups (i.e., to challenge students' reasoning and to prepare them to confront difficult decision-making situations). The leader also identified group guidelines for matters such as confidentiality, attendance, and discussion of personal journals.

Session 2. Members talked about why they wanted to participate in a dilemma discussion group related to drug use and abuse. They discussed the role peer pressure plays in drug use and how television advertisements encourage use of alcohol and other drugs. Students also considered the possible use of warning labels on alcoholic beverages as a deterrent to abuse.

Session 3. Students reflected on their journal entries about the previous session. Next, the leader offered opportunities for members to discuss not only what they knew about drugs but also how they felt about various kinds of drugs, including legal and illegal drugs used for recreational purposes. Finally, the leader presented students with information about consequences of abusing drugs and encouraged students to discuss their feelings about the short-term and long-term consequences of drug use.

Session 4. This session began with students reflecting on their journal entries and reviewing the consequences of substance abuse. Next, the group leader presented students with their first drug-related dilemma for discussion.

> Jim had just moved and was enrolled in his new high school. He hated the thought of having to make all new friends. He was shy, and kids passed him in the halls as if he didn't exist. He thought the kids at his new school were unfriendly. He didn't know anyone. Most of the time he wanted to stay home on school days.
>
> Today, a guy named Bill from math class asked Jim to eat with him. Lunch was great. Jim enjoyed telling Bill about his old school, and Bill seemed interested. Jim looked forward to having a new friend.
>
> When they left the cafeteria, Bill said "I've noticed that nobody talks to you. You always eat lunch by yourself. I've got something here in my backpack that will make you forget about the unfriendly kids here." Bill showed Jim what was in his backpack and smiled knowingly.
>
> Jim, feeling embarrassed and confused, said nothing.
>
> "No rush, Jim, they'll keep," Bill said. "See you later," and he walked off.
>
> Jim wanted a friend, but he wasn't sure if he wanted to get involved in drugs. What should Jim do?

The leader asked students to reflect on Jim's dilemma and to consider questions, such as what are Jim's choices, what will he probably decide to do, and how might other students have helped to prevent Jim's dilemma?

Session 5. Students began this session by reflecting on journal entries about their first dilemma discussion. Typical student comments included "I would never be friends with Bill. He's just looking to take advantage of a new kid" and "Jim needs to talk with his parents so that Bill will not ruin his life." Following this discussion the leader presented another dilemma for group members to consider. Students discussed the new dilemma and role-played various interactions suggested in the dilemma. During and following the role-play, the leader posed questions challenging students' thinking.

Session 6. Following review of the dilemmas presented in the previous session, the leader asked students to consider how to write their own drug-related dilemmas. They discussed the main components of the previous dilemmas, including (a) focus on a genuine problem, (b) action centering on a main character, (c) the presence of choice that has no apparent correct answer, and (d) a question posed about what the main character in the dilemma should do (Galbraith & Jones, 1976).

Session 7. After briefly reflecting on their journal entries about the previous session, students discussed how it felt to write dilemmas on their own. Those who did not write dilemmas participated in the discussion and talked about feelings that led them not to complete the assignment. The discussion was frank and included comments such as "Dilemmas are easy to write if they don't come from your own life," "I hate to write," and "I like writing my own dilemmas because they are real and don't sound made up."

Session 8. Following review of the previous session and discussion of journal entries, the leader organized students into small groups to write dilemmas during the session. The leader circulated among the groups, encouraging them to stay on task and to complete dilemmas for consideration at the next session.

Session 9. Students read and discussed some of the dilemmas they had written in Session 8. The dilemmas covered situations such as older siblings encouraging drug use, having easy access to wine and beer at home, and trying drugs at weekend parties. The leader assigned the writing of one more personal dilemma as homework and urged everyone to try to complete the assignment.

Session 10. Students reflected briefly on their journal entries and then discussed the dilemmas they were assigned to write. At this point in the group process, some of the dilemmas were quite personal and sometimes difficult for students to discuss. As students read and discussed their dilemmas, the group leader and group members asked challenging questions and expressed empathy for the difficult situation presented.

Session 11. At the beginning of this session, the leader asked students to read through each of their journal entries from the previous sessions. Students discussed the progress (or lack of progress) in their thinking about drug dilemmas. The leader invited students who felt they had made progress to describe their feelings for all in the group to hear. The leader then encouraged participants who saw no movement in their own thinking to discuss their feelings and to consider how their thinking might change in the future.

Session 12. Students listed and discussed positive attributes of each group member and the group leader. They also suggested changes for future groups of this kind, including to make sure that all dilemmas were real (or at least sounded real) and to encourage quiet group members to talk more.

The elements incorporated into these group sessions were based on characteristics of successful Deliberate Psychological Education programs (Thies-Sprinthall, 1984). These elements included (a) challenging students' current conceptions and cognitive levels related to drug dilemmas, (b) providing role-taking experiences that allowed students to consider the perspectives of peers, and (c) providing students opportunities to reflect on thoughts and feelings about drug-related issues.

Pre- and Postmeasures of Students' Reasoning and Conceptual Levels. Two measures were chosen to assess changes in reasoning and conceptual level: the *Defining Issues Test* (DIT) developed by Rest (1979) and the *Paragraph Completion Test* (PCT) developed by Hunt (1971). The first of these measures, the DIT, evaluates the basic conceptual framework that individuals use in analyzing social and moral problems and in choosing appropriate courses of action. During the test participants read dilemmas, decide what action should be taken by the principal figure in the dilemmas, rank 12 statements as to their importance in the course of action chosen, and then list the 4 most relevant of the 12 statements. Responses to the dilemmas yield scores that may be converted to indicate the percentage of student reasoning at Level 1 (preconventional), Level 2 (conventional), or Level 3 (postconventional, principled). As Sprinthall and Collins (1984) have explained, (a) preconventional moral reasoning is based in "external, quasi-physical happenings, in bad acts, or in quasi-physical needs rather than in persons and standards"; (b) conventional reasoning is based in "performing good or right roles, in maintaining the conventional order, and in meeting others' expectations"; and (c) postconventional reasoning is based in "principles that can be applied universally" (p. 179). This study concerned itself only with changes in the percentage of postconventional or principled thought resulting from the drug abuse prevention program.

The complete DIT provides participants with six dilemmas to read. For the purposes of this study, a shorter, three-dilemma version was administered. Scores on the shorter version have a correlation of .93 with scores on the complete DIT. Test–retest reliability for the DIT has ranged from .70 to .80 with internal consistency reliability about .80. The DIT has been shown to have high levels of concurrent validity (correlations ranging from .20 to .50 with variables such as achievement, aptitude, and IQ), construct validity (correlations ranging from .40 to .70 on variables such as cognitive ability and comprehension of moral values), and criterion-group validity (Davidson & Robbins, 1978).

The second measure of reasoning used in this study, the PCT, consists of sentence stems to which individuals respond with written personal reactions. These sentence stems include:

> What I think about rules . . .
> When I am criticized . . .
> What I think about parents . . .
> When someone does not agree with me . . .
> When I'm not sure . . .
> When I'm told what to do . . .

Trained raters using clinical judgment evaluate the conceptual level of responses. Raters assign a score of 0 to 3 to each of the six responses to the sentence stems. A conceptual level is calculated by averaging the three highest scores. Scores have the following meanings: (a) A score of 0 indicates an undifferentiated response that excludes negative input and lacks affective control, (b) a score of 1 indicates categorical judgments with heavy reliance on a single rule with recourse to external standards, (c) a score of 2 indicates some form of conditional evaluation with recognition of alternative responses, and (d) a score of 3 indicates the consideration of two viewpoints and clear reliance on internal standards.

The interrater reliability of trained raters varies from .80 to .95. The PCT has been extensively studied (Hunt, 1971) and has been shown to have correlations with intelligence (ranging from .09 to .29), with age and grade (ranging from .08 to .17), with academic achievement (ranging from .16 to .17), and with personality measures (ranging from .12 to .34). Studies have further shown that individuals with high conceptual levels as measured by the PCT seem to score low on measures of prejudice (Gardiner, 1972) and score high on measures of internal locus of control (McLachlan, 1972).

Results

Changes in Principled Reasoning

Table 1 shows the changes in percentage of principled reasoning as measured on the DIT. The data in this table were analyzed by multiple analysis of variance comparing gains for students in each of the groups.

TABLE 1
ANOVA on Pretreatment and Posttreatment Changes in Percentage of Principled Reasoning as Measured by the Defining Issues Test

Groups	Pretreatment		Posttreatment		ANOVA	
	M	SD	M	SD	F	p
Experimental Group 1 ($n = 14$)	13.09	8.10	24.50	10.60	11.90	< .05
Experimental Group 2 ($n = 14$)	18.29	11.50	27.39	13.50		
Control group ($n = 24$)	12.22	7.40	11.94	8.00		

A Tukey post hoc analysis was used to determine the source of statistical significance. The Tukey method was chosen because, as Einot and Gabriel (1975) and Keppel (1982) have shown, it is more powerful than other methods for pair-wise tests.

Participants in both experimental groups showed increases in percentage of principled reasoning. Experimental group 1 had a mean gain of 11.41% in principled reasoning, and group 2 had a mean gain of 9.1%. Controls showed a mean decline of 0.28% in principled reasoning. The changes in principled reasoning were significant, $F = 11.90$, $p < .05$, with significant differences between the experimental groups and controls. There was no statistical difference between Experimental group 1 and Experimental group 2 in gains in principled reasoning.

Further analysis was conducted within the two experimental groups to determine if any participants declined in percentage of principled thought from pre- to posttreatment and to determine if any developmental patterns emerged (i.e., if students at lower pretreatment levels of principled thinking benefited similarly to students at higher pretreatment levels). This additional analysis revealed that no participants in the drug prevention program decreased in their percentage of principled thinking and that no developmental patterns emerged. Among the 28 members in the two experimental groups the following occurred: (a) Ten students gained from 0% to 5% in principled thought (the pretreatment percentage of principled thought for these students

TABLE 2
ANOVA on Pretreatment and Posttreatment Changes in Conceptual Level as Measured by the Paragraph Completion Test

Groups	Pretreatment		Posttreatment		ANOVA	
	M	SD	M	SD	F	p
Experimental Group 1 ($n = 14$)	1.17	0.39	1.29	0.37	2.60	NS
Experimental Group 2 ($n = 14$)	1.06	0.40	1.35	0.38		
Control group ($n = 24$)	1.17	0.44	1.06	0.43		

NS = nonsignificant.

ranged from 10.00 to 40.00, with a mean of 23.66%), (b) 4 students gained from 6% to 10% in principled thought (the pretreatment percentage of principled thought for these students ranged from 3.33 to 26.66, with a mean of 12.85%), and (c) 11 students gained 11% or more in principled thought (the pretreatment percentage of principled thought for these students ranged from 6.66 to 23.33, with a mean of 15.11%).

The pretest differences across the preceding three subgroups within the experimental group thus did not predict who would gain from the intervention. There was only a 3-point difference on the initial level of reasoned judgment according to students who showed very little, a moderate, or a large gain in posttest scores. This indicates that the general approach to dilemma discussion in the study was appropriate to the range of students who participated in the experimental groups.

Changes in Conceptual Level

Table 2 shows the changes in conceptual level as measured by the PCT. The data in this table were also analyzed by multiple analysis of variance comparing pre- to postgains for students in each of the groups.

Participants in both experimental groups showed small increases in conceptual level. Experimental group 1 had a mean gain of 0.12, and group 2 had a mean gain of 0.29. Controls showed a mean decline of 0.11 in conceptual level. None of the differences was statistically significant.

Discussion

This study posed the following question: Will a drug abuse prevention curriculum that challenges students' thinking about drug use through discussion and reflection on drug-related dilemmas promote the process of individuation among adolescents by advancing students' moral reasoning and increasing their conceptual level? The results suggest a qualified "yes" response, indicating that a short-term, dilemma discussion approach to drug education can increase levels of principled thinking in adolescents as measured by the DIT but is unlikely to increase conceptual level as measured by the PCT.

The measures themselves actually tap into quite different levels of cognitive structural change. The Rest DIT requires that students improve their awareness of judgment issues. The students pick out the system of reasoning that they might use in dilemma situations. They are not required to produce their own ideas or reasons. In a sense, then, the DIT may be considered as measuring a first step in developmental growth. The students who participated in the experimental classes demonstrated a preference for samples of higher level reasoning. This is also referred to as the "Plus One" phenomenon, which is to appreciate and select slightly more complex reasons.

The Hunt PCT measure, on the other hand, requires that the students use their own works to demonstrate higher level reasoning. To complete the sentence stems in the PCT involves a projection of actual thought process rather than a recognition from a list of reasons. From this view the Hunt instrument can be considered as a measure of deeper or more fundamental cognitive structural growth, which is presumably more resistant to change. We may, therefore, suggest that whereas a relatively short-term program raises student consciousness concerning reasoning about difficult issues, a program of longer duration may be required to create deeper structural changes in cognition. More extensive time and additional experiences may be necessary to help students incorporate (or, in Piaget's term, to accommodate) the more complex thinking skills into their emergent cognitions. Further research is obviously needed to test programs that may accomplish both goals of raising consciousness and of modifying cognitive structures.

An additional finding of this study revealed that no participants in the drug education program decreased their percentage of principled thinking from pre- to posttreatment. This finding is important because of concerns sometimes voiced by parents and teachers suggesting that drug education may be harmful, causing students to be less mature in their judgments about experimenting with drugs and alcohol. Although these concerns were undoubtedly justified in regard to early drug education programs designed primarily to dispense information about drugs, the concerns seem unfounded in relation to programs of the type described in this study. Parents and teachers may have confidence in drug education efforts that incorporate elements of Deliberate Psychological Education programs that include challenging students' current conceptions and cognitive levels related to drug dilemmas, providing role-taking experiences that allow students to consider the perspectives of peers, and providing students opportunities to reflect on thoughts and feelings about drug-related issues.

This study leaves some important issues unsettled. It does not, for example, clearly show the value of tailoring drug education curricula to the specific developmental levels of individual students. The amount of growth students achieved in this study was unrelated to their developmental level as measured in pretesting. Earlier studies (Hedin, 1979; Thies-Sprinthall, 1984), in contrast, have demonstrated the advantages of differentiated focus on participants at different initial stages of development. Hunt (1971) has also proposed the need for a manageable mismatch between students' current levels of development and educational interventions, suggesting that too great a discrepancy between student development and educational programming results in a developmental version of "ships passing in the night." The short-term nature of the drug education program involved in this study may account for the lack of developmental pattern in the growth resulting from the intervention.

Conclusion

Although this study's outcomes must be viewed cautiously in light of the small number of students participating, the study shows that drug-related dilemma discussions may in a very short time raise student consciousness about the crucial issues involved in whether or not to use drugs. The study suggests further, however, that more intense programs of longer duration may be required to make deeper changes in students' cognitive structures. The short-term program studied here is a first step in the process of developing drug abuse prevention programs that will promote structural changes in cognition necessary for students to make mature decisions about drug use, decisions less influenced by peer pressure.

References

Carter, D. (1983, October). Why do kids use drugs and alcohol, and how do we help them stop? *PTA Today*, p. 25.

Davidson, M., & Robbins, S. (1978). The reliability and validity of objective indices of moral development. *Applied Psychological Measurement, 2*, 391–403.

Einot, I., & Gabriel, K. R. (1975). A study of power of several methods of multiple comparisons. *Journal of the American Statistical Association, 70*, 574–583.

Galbraith, R. E., & Jones, T. M. (1976). *Moral reasoning: A teaching handbook for adapting Kohlberg to the classroom.* Anoka, MN: Greenhaven Press, Inc.

Gardiner, G. (1972). Complexity training and prejudice reduction. *Journal of Applied Social Psychology, 2*, 326–342.

Gerler, E. R. (1986). Skills for adolescence: A new program for young teenagers. *Phi Delta Kappan, 67*, 436–439.

Hedin, D. (1979). *Teenage health education: An action learning program to promote development.* Unpublished doctoral thesis, University of Minnesota, Minneapolis.

Horan, J. J., & Williams, J. M. (1982). Longitudinal study of assertion training as a drug abuse prevention strategy. *American Educational Research Journal, 19*, 341–351.

Hunt, D. (1971). *Matching models in education.* Toronto, Ontario: Ontario Institute for Studies in Education.

Keppel, G. (1982). *Design and analysis: A researcher's handbook.* Englewood Cliffs, NJ: Prentice-Hall.

Kohlberg, L. (1979). *Measuring moral judgment.* Worcester, MA: Clark University Press.

Loevinger, J. (1977). *Ego development.* San Francisco, CA: Jossey-Bass.

McLachlan, J. (1972). Benefits from group therapy as a function of patient-therapist match on conceptual level. *Psychotherapy: Theory, Research, & Practice, 9*, 317–323.

Mohr, P. H., Sprinthall, N. A., & Gerler, E. R. (1987). Moral reasoning in early adolescence: Implications for drug abuse prevention. *School Counselor, 35*, 120–127.

Rest, J. (1979). *Manual for the Defining Issues Test.* University of Minnesota, Minneapolis.

Selman, R. (1980). *The growth of interpersonal understanding.* New York: Academic Press.

Sprinthall, N. A., & Collins, W. A. (1984). *Adolescent psychology: A developmental view.* Reading, MA: Addison-Wesley.

Thies-Sprinthall, L. (1984). Promoting the developmental growth of supervising teachers: Theory, research, programs, and implications. *Journal of Teacher Education, 35,* 53–60.

PART THREE

SAMPLE DEVELOPMENTAL LESSON PLANS

Introduction to Part Three

The chapters in Part Three (chapters 9 –14) provide sample lesson plans that can be incorporated into developmental interventions. The plans are organized in six content areas appropriate for school counselor involvement. These plans are not offered to be used in isolation. Instead, they should be used as a part of carefully developed programs similar to those described in chapters 6–8.

The lessons are designed to teach children and adolescents at all developmental levels that they have power, that they can learn appropriate skills, and that they can make effective and responsible decisions. The chapters encourage counselors to write clear educational goals and objectives that are developmentally appropriate.

With any of these topics, awareness of developmental principles can assist counselors in adapting the length and style of the presentations, as well as the vocabulary to meet individual student needs. Counselors can choose strategies that have been shown to be successful in promoting development. Dilemma discussions and sharing of the children's personal experiences will allow students to hear the reasoning of their classmates. Children at higher levels of development can provide the plus-one reasoning needed by others in the class. The facilitation skills of the counselor can be especially helpful in eliciting multilevel responses.

Each chapter provides introductory principles and rationales, broad K–12 goals for these areas, sample objectives by age groups, and sample lesson plans. The lesson plans are included as *examples* of the types of activities that might be part of an ongoing developmental intervention integrated within academic curricula. It is recommended that the counselor develop an overall sequence that emphasizes different objectives or competencies at each grade level. Integrating counseling goals with academic goals should be attempted whenever possible. This collaboration might involve joint planning, serving as a guest speaker, or providing resources to teachers.

Assessing the outcomes of interventions is also important. Sometimes a simple quiz on specific content can provide useful information. Other times, evaluation of the process by the students can refine interventions. In addition, children and adolescents can be asked to engage in self-assessment through journaling or responding to monitoring sheets. These activities offer an opportunity for students to reflect on experience—a necessary component for development.

Beyond classroom and small-group interventions, counselors can also address all of these topics through total school programs. Peer helper programs, service clubs, academic booster clubs, and special recognition programs can all provide opportunities for significant role-taking experiences for students. Community projects can enhance self-esteem and encourage a sense of responsibility.

The areas addressed in these next chapters need to be considered as appropriate areas for preventive and deliberate psychological education within schools. They provide content areas through which environments and experiences can be provided to promote development. The suggestions presented here are intended only as a beginning—to stimulate thought and creativity and to encourage purposeful planning and assessment.

CHAPTER 9

School Success

Introduction

Counselors have an important role involving the use of developmental principles and educational needs in designing programs to meet cognitive as well as affective objectives in helping children progress through various developmental stages. For example, Hunt's ideas about conceptual level can provide a framework for understanding young people as learners. Counselors need to work cooperatively with the entire school staff in integrating programs that meet these academic needs, being aware that self-esteem is an important component of learning, but that it cannot be dealt with in a vacuum apart from the academic program of the school.

Goals

Children and adolescents will:

- Become oriented to the school environment
- Learn effective study skills and test-taking strategies
- Develop critical thinking skills
- Identify academic strengths, weaknesses, and individual learning styles

- Develop skill in making educational decisions
- Understand their role in group process
- Develop responsible behaviors within the classroom

Sample Objectives

The following are sample objectives by grade level. Each objective is introduced at the earliest possible level, and it is assumed that this objective will continue to be important at higher levels without being repeated in later lists.

K–5 children will demonstrate ability and skills in regard to:

- Behaving appropriately in group activities
- Using effective listening skills
- Using self-control and accepting individual responsibility
- Understanding the importance of learning
- Following instructions, completing assignments, and working independently
- Learning how to prepare for testing situations
- Setting short-term educational goals
- Describing information they can learn about themselves from taking a test
- Distinguishing between fact and opinion
- Recognizing differences in the way they learn for different subjects, settings, and objectives

Middle school children will demonstrate ability and skills in regard to:

- Using appropriate methods for studying and test taking
- Asserting themselves by asking questions
- Becoming aware of importance of middle school performance to future educational choices
- Identifying what motivates them to perform well and understanding the relationship between effort and learning
- Recognizing how attitudes influence learning
- Demonstrating the ability to plan their own study time
- Applying appropriate educational decision-making skills, including developing a tentative 4-year education plan
- Recognizing individual academic strengths and weaknesses

- Implementing effective study and test-taking skills
- Evaluating the importance of balancing study time and extra-curricular activities
- Learning responsible behaviors within the classroom, school, and community

High school students will demonstrate ability and skills in regard to:

- Becoming aware of the importance of high school performance to future plans
- Applying appropriate educational decision-making skills and learning to set priorities
- Recognizing individual academic strengths and weaknesses
- Implementing a 4-year education plan and revising as needed
- Demonstrating the ability to set short-term and long-term educational goals
- Understanding how success and failure are a normal part of life and learning
- Realizing that learning is achieved in small sequential steps and that it is wise to focus on the small step
- Recognizing how peers influence attitudes toward learning and dealing appropriately with peer influences
- Assessing the skills needed to cope with changing job markets
- Understanding the importance of academic skills for achieving desired life-style, standard of living, and occupational choices
- Analyzing and comparing their achievements with those skills necessary for short-range and long-range planning

Sample Lesson Plans

The following lesson plans are designed to provide examples of the types of specific activities that could be incorporated into an ongoing classroom counseling unit or integrated within academic curricula. They are chosen to deal with a particular developmental task or event or to offer opportunities for growth. However, counselors are encouraged to remember that developmental programs to foster school success involve long-term interventions to meet K–12 goals and objectives. School-wide programs such as peer tutoring or facilitation and academic booster clubs can assist in encouraging appropriate levels of responsibility and promoting development.

The Berenstain Bears Go to School

Grade Level: Kindergarten
Objective: To assist in orienting students to the school environment
Time: 30 minutes
Type of Activity: Classroom counseling session conducted during the first 2 weeks of school
Materials Needed: A copy of *The Berenstain Bears Go to School* by Stan and Jan Berenstain (NY: Random House, 1978)
Procedure: Read the book to the class. The story is about Sister Bear starting kindergarten and tells about her feelings, experiences, and adjustments. After reading the book, ask basic recall questions to anchor the information for students. Then try the following processs questions:

> Did you ever feel like Sister Bear?
> What has been fun about being in school?
> What are you looking forward to about the school year?

These questions are designed to let students talk about their feelings and to think positively about school. With hope, this story will be used in conjunction with other activities to help students become comfortable in the school environment. Other activities could include a tour of the school or a "big brother/big sister" program using older elementary students as special friends. Meetings with key people in the school, such as the principal, secretary, librarian, custodian, and lunchroom staff, can also help children start to feel at home.

Developed By: Leslie Martin Rainey, Doctoral Candidate, School Counseling

Willie McGurgle

Grade Level: 4th
Objective: To encourage the use of effective listening skills
Time: 30 minutes

Type of Activity: Classroom counseling session
Materials Needed: A copy of the poem "Willie McGurgle" (author unknown)
Drawing paper and crayons
Procedure: Remind students of the importance of listening carefully. Then read the poem:

> Did you ever hear of Willie McGurgle
> Who limped around town with his nose painted purple?
> He was the ugliest man I ever have seen!
> One eye was orange and the other was green.
> Yellow hair hung down like straw on his head.
> He dressed all in brown with patches of red.
> Out of his beat up shoes, his poor toes stuck through.
> In very cold weather, his toes turned blue.
> One day in the rain, beneath an umbrella of black,
> Willie left town and he never came back.

Have students attempt to draw Willie as close to their memory of his description as possible. When everyone has finished, read the poem again slowly and let the students "check" their own work.
Developed By: Leslie Martin Rainey, Doctoral Candidate, School Counseling

Today Was a Terrible Day

Grade Level: 5th
Objective: To understand the importance of learning
Time: 40 minutes
Type of Activity: Classroom session
Materials Needed: A copy of *Today Was a Terrible Day* by Patricia Giff (NY: Viking, 1982; Puffin Books, 1984)
Procedure: Introduce the story by asking students if they have ever had a really bad day at school. Tell them that you are going to read them a story about a very bad day that Ronald Morgan had. Read the story. The story is about Ronald Morgan who has all kinds of things go wrong including being nicknamed and insulted because he can't read well. His understanding teacher helps him regain his confidence through her encouraging words.

DEVELOPMENTAL SCHOOL COUNSELING PROGRAMS

Ask students the following process questions:

What did you notice about the story?
How did you feel about what happened to Ronald?
Did the story remind you of anything in our school?

Students could also be asked to write encouraging notes to each other or a "thank-you" note to someone who had encouraged them.

Adapted From: A lesson plan by Sarah Borders, EdS, School Counseling

Study Skills: Test Jeopardy

Grade Levels: 6th–8th
Objectives: To learn effective study skills and test-taking strategies
To encourage effective time management and test preparation
Time: 30 minutes
Type of Activity: Classroom session
Materials Needed: "Jeopardy" board, index cards, pencils
Procedure: Introduce yourself and the session on study skills.
Highlight the importance of study habits and effort to performance and grades.
Discuss different types of tests and various purposes from classroom tests to driver's tests.
Explain that you will take a closer look at study skills and specifically test preparation and test taking today to determine strategies for improving grades.
Brainstorm a list of study tips and test-taking strategies.
Organize the class into three to four smaller teams; instruct these groups to come up with Jeopardy questions for the specific categories listed and to write them on the index cards.
Allow 8–10 minutes and collect questions and combine with yours.
Spend the remaining time playing Jeopardy and have game board or use chalkboard.

Suggestions:	This is a fun and interactive classroom activity that students love.
I recommend preparing the Jeopardy playing board beforehand.
This will require selecting specific categories and then you can ask questions according to these content areas.
Developed By:	Lisa Murray, MA, School Counseling

My Way

Grade Levels:	6th–8th
Objective:	To help students evaluate their present study habits and to recognize their individual academic strengths and weaknesses
Time:	30 minutes
Type of Activity:	Classroom session
Materials Needed:	Pencil and paper
Procedure:	Introduce yourself and the session discussing study habits.
Include any specifics relating to this group and their school situation (i.e., time during grading period). Discuss the relationship between effort and learning and how attitudes influence learning. Emphasize that each student has a unique approach to learning and his or her own study habits.
Think about the following activities and how you approach them. What are the positive (+) and productive methods that are helpful and effective study skills? What are some of the negative (-) or unproductive methods that interfere with your school success?
List them under each activity:

  Doing homework
  Reviewing for a test
  Listening to a lecture
  Doing a report
  Following directions
  (any others you select) |

	Using the information listed, discuss orally or in writing a few strengths and weaknesses as a student. Write a short- and long-term goal (1 week and 4 weeks) and an appropriate reward.
Suggestions for Teachers:	Students may do this individually, in small groups, or as a class. Review the personal academic goals and offer an appropriate reward.
Developed By:	Lisa Murray, MA, School Counseling

Who Makes the Rules?

Grade Levels:	6th and 7th
Objectives:	To help orient students to school rules and acceptable school behaviors
	To teach students to accept responsibility for their behavior and resulting consequences
Time:	30 minutes
Type of Activity:	Classroom or Small Group
Materials Needed:	Pencil and paper
	School Handbook
Procedure:	Introduce yourself and unit on School Rules, Behaviors and Consequences. Prepare several true/false questions related to school rules. Instruct students to stand if they believe the answer is true and to remain seated if they believe it is false. Ideas may cover classroom conduct, lunch privileges, or consequences for cutting class or being disrespectful. Identify and list as many school rules and norms that you can.
	Working in pairs have the students prepare a problem statement or concern they would like to address about school rules. Collect these and pass out a role slip to each student—either "student," "classroom teacher," or "principal."
	Divide according to these roles and explain that the "students" will have the anonymous concerns/problems/questions to direct to the appropriate adult group.

Suggestions for Teachers:	Allow the groups a few minutes to assume their roles and prepare to explain and clarify potential rule questions.

The design allows you to hand pick particular students for the various roles and structure the ground rules accordingly.

This activity can serve as subject for a writing assignment or poll of other students regarding school rules. |
| Developed By: | Lisa Murray, MA, School Counseling |

What Will I Do After I Graduate?

Grade Level:	10th
Objectives:	To learn how to utilize a decision-making process
To realistically explore alternatives for the future
Time:	40 minutes
Type of Activity:	Classroom counseling session
Materials Needed:	Chalkboard
Procedure:	This unit is presented in a lecture/discussion format. Write the following career decision-making process steps on the board and explain them.
1. Define the problem—Ask the class what the problem is (what will I do after I graduate?).
2. Define the goals—Ask the class for the goal (to decide what to do after graduation).
3. Obtain information—Have students write their answers:
*About self—What are your interests, abilities, skills, strengths, weaknesses? What do you need to be happy? Inform students that they will need to think more about this outside of class.
*About careers—How much education will you need? What type of work environment (around people/by yourself)? Do you want to work regular hours? Where do you want to live? Tell students to check in the library or guidance office, or talk to people in the field to obtain more information.

4. Select alternatives—job, technical school, community college, or 4-year college.
5. Weigh alternatives—Ask several students to share careers that are of interest to them. With each response, ask if the student has the interest and skills and knows what the career entails—reality check!
6. Tentative decision—At this point, what do you think you want to do after you graduate?
7. Implement decision or recycle—What's your next step (e.g., take classes that would help you in your career; i.e., accounting if you want to be a CPA, shop if you want to be a welder)? Send for information about colleges and trade schools.

Developed By: Katharine Simmons, MA, School Counseling

What College or Technical School Will I Choose?

Grade Level: 11th or early 12th
Objectives: To aid students in more wisely and thoroughly selecting higher education settings
To help students choose institutions that are consistent with their career goals
Time: 40 minutes
Type of Activity: Classroom counseling session
Materials Needed: Blackboard
Procedure: Ask students to list several occupations in which they have interest, then have them list the higher educational institutions they are considering.
Have several students share their career goals. Ask what their tentative colleges are and if they are the type of institutions that will help them reach these goals (curriculum, degrees offered, etc.).
Ask students what their bases for choosing schools are (e.g., cost, amount of financial aid available, campus size, faculty–student ratio, courses offered, strength of their departments of interest, geographical location, ethnic diversity, reputation, support services, etc.). If students do not have this infor-

mation, suggest that they later go to the library or guidance office for answers.

Ask for one student volunteer to be used as an example for making a tentative college decision. Have that student share his or her top four schools and his or her four major criteria in choosing a school. Using the following chart format on the blackboard, have the student assess each criterion for each school and rank each school according to it. Give the school that the student considers to have the highest rank a 4, then correspondingly 3, 2, and 1. Multiply that number by the row number (e.g., if School C ranks highest in Criterion 4, under School C write 16 (4 x 4); if School A ranks lowest in Criterion 3, in that section write 3 (3 x 1). After going through all the criteria, total the columns. The school with the highest number should be the student's first choice. Carry on a question-and-answer section. Students have many questions concerning colleges, and this will provide an opportunity for them to receive answers.

	School A	School B	School C	School D
(strongest) criterion 5				
criterion 4				
criterion 3				
criterion 2				
(weakest) criterion 1				

Remind students that this process is not limited to school selection, but may be utilized for many types of decisions.

Developed By: Katharine Simmons, MA, School Counseling

Give Me an A (or a B?)

Grade Level: 9th
Objective: To improve study skills and grades
Time: 1 hour

Type of Activity: Classroom counseling session
Materials Needed: Chalkboard
Procedure: This unit is presented in a lecture/discussion format.

Introduce the purpose and concept of study skills (more efficient studying and better grades). Mention that the ability to study efficiently and effectively is not something we're born with, but something we learn and, with practice, become even better at.

Ask if anyone has ever felt "bummed out" because he or she studied hard for a test, but still got a lower grade than he or she had expected. Ask: How did that affect you? Did you study even harder or just give up because you felt it wasn't worth the effort?

Discuss the following study tips with the class:

1. The time to worry about grades isn't right before you get your report card. Why? When?
2. Know your strengths and weaknesses in terms of studying, and spend more time on the subjects that are hard for you. Also, study your hardest subjects first while your mind is more alert.
3. Teachers are your greatest resource—they're there to help as long as you're willing to work. Go to them (a) as soon as you have a problem/don't understand, (b) before a test if you're confused, and (c) after a test—they can help point out your areas of weakness and where you need to/how you can improve.
4. Ask questions in class—chances are good that others don't understand either, and you'd be doing them a favor, too.
5. Get a tutor—this doesn't mean you're a "wimp" (where and how can you find a tutor?).
6. Set realistic goals in terms of grades and stick to them! If you're good in English, decide to make an A and challenge yourself! If physics is very difficult for you, maybe set your goal

as a C—if this is the absolute *best* you can do. Remember that not everyone's a real whiz in every subject, and that as long as you try your hardest, you're a winner—even if your best friend gets a higher grade.
7. Check your notebook with a friend's to see if you've missed anything.
8. If you can stay on task while studying with someone, this is a good way to study for a test. Ask each other questions.
9. Make up possible test questions and answer them.
10. Don't wait until the last minute to study for a test—for most people, information ends up jumbled in their brains and they blank out on the answers.
11. If you're alert during a test you'll do better, so get a good night's sleep and eat a good breakfast the morning of the test.

Developed By: Katharine Simmons, MA, School Counseling

CHAPTER 10

Effective Problem Solving

Introduction

Educators have tried for generations to teach children to make appropriate decisions. However, conflicts developed when children and adolescents made decisions that adults did not like. Although the spoken words said, "You are capable of making effective decisions," the unspoken message was all too often, "You'd better do as I say and accept decisions adults make for you." This becomes increasingly confusing to young people as they reach higher developmental levels. It is much easier for young people to do as they are told and avoid decision making, especially because this absolves them of responsibility for the outcome. How much easier it is to blame parents, teachers, or others if plans go awry. Adults often fail to notice children's higher stages of development and continue to treat them as if they were not capable of higher level thinking skills. But this approach backfires when parents and teachers realize—often too late—that young people are swept away by peer pressure. Children who have never been allowed to select their clothing because of a parental fear that their clothes might not be perfectly matched will not learn overnight to make appropriate decisions about alcohol, drugs, or sex. Suddenly a wonderfully obedient child has changed from obeying parents and teachers to following mindlessly under the influence of peers. Suddenly adults are saying to young people, "Why don't you make decisions for yourself?"

Stage theorists can help adults understand the developmental needs of young people as they grow in ability to make increasingly complex decisions. For example, Kohlberg's work on moral reasoning can help adults understand the simplicity of younger children's reasoning and can provide opportunities for children to move gradually torward more complex decision making. Hunt's conceptual levels give us a way to understand children and adolescents as learners. Using this framework, adults can anticipate needs for structure and provide environments and experiences that represent constructive mismatches. One of the potent effects of using these theories is to sensitize adults to the fact that children need to have opportunities for increasingly complex decision making. For example, it seems obvious that children cannot progress appropriately through stages involving Erikson's concepts of mastery versus inferiority and identity versus diffusion if they are denied opportunities to make decisions that demonstrate mastery and show that they can do so separately and confidently as individuals, rather than as extensions of parents or teachers.

School counselors have an important opportunity to show young people that effective decision making can lead to greater self-esteem and responsibility. Additionally, they can demonstrate to teachers that children cannot develop faith in their own decision making unless adults provide opportunities, support, and guidance in the process. Counselors can provide materials to assist teachers in this process, and can help promote this type of development by helping teachers integrate decision-making lessons throughout the curriculum.

Goals

Children and adolescents will:

- Develop a sense of personal responsibility
- Learn effective decision-making skills
- Learn to set short-term goals
- Learn to evaluate the effects of decisions
- Learn to distinguish between facts and assumptions

Sample Objectives

The following are sample objectives by grade level. Each objective is introduced at the earliest possible level, and it is assumed that this objective will continue to be important at higher levels without being repeated in later lists.

K–5 children will demonstrate ability and skills in regard to:

- Recognizing the importance of self-control
- Describing choices they make at school
- Describing responsibilities they have at home and at school
- Describing decisions they make and describing those that others make for them
- Recognizing that decisions have consequences
- Discussing ways to solve problems with friends
- Understanding a decision-making/problem-solving process
- Understanding the problem-solving model and conflict-resolution strategies

Middle grade students will demonstrate ability and skills in regard to:

- Applying problem-solving skills to conflict situations
- Evaluating how listening and talking accurately helps to solve problems
- Providing examples of how past decisions have affected present actions
- Distinguishing between personal wants and needs
- Demonstrating a sense of control and responsibility for personal behavior
- Evaluating how responsibility helps them manage their lives

High school students will demonstrate ability and skills in regard to:

- Learning to identify their responsible/irresponsible behaviors
- Distinguishing between self-defeating and self-enhancing behaviors
- Differentiating between healthy and unhealthy solutions to problems
- Recognizing that solutions to problems cannot always be ideal
- Learning to make decisions that are in their own best interests
- Recognizing the degree of personal control over problems
- Applying decision-making skills to personal goal setting
- Learning about procrastination and how it applies to decision making

Sample Lesson Plans

The following lesson plans are designed to provide examples of the types of specific activities that could be incorporated into an ongoing classroom counseling unit or integrated within academic curricula. They are chosen to deal with a particular developmental task or event or to offer opportunities for growth. However, counselors are encouraged to remember that developmental programs to foster effective problem solving involve long-term interventions to meet K–12 goals and objectives. School-wide programs such as conflict mediation and shared decision making can assist in encouraging appropriate levels of responsibility and promoting development.

That's What Friends Are For

Grade Levels: K–1st
Objective: To demonstrate alternate forms of problem solving
Time: 30 minutes
Type of Activity: Classroom or small-group session
Materials Needed: A copy of *That's What Friends Are For* by Florence Parry Heide and Sylvia Worth Van Clief (NY: Scholastics Books Service, 1968)
Procedure: Read the story of Theodore, an elephant with a hurt leg, who cannot go to the edge of the jungle to meet his cousin. Theodore meets many of his animal friends who try to offer their own solutions to the problem. The bird suggests flying, the monkey thinks swinging by your tail from tree to tree would be the best, and so on. None of their solutions works for Theodore. They "put their heads together" and come up with another idea that does work.
The other animals go meet Theodore's cousin and bring him into the jungle.
Ask students if they have ever had a problem someone else helped them solve. [Let them briefly share.] Then introduce a very simple problem-solving model.

EFFECTIVE PROBLEM SOLVING

> Name the problem.
> Brainstorm solutions.
> Think about what might work.
> Pick a solution and try it.
>
> Ask students to think of a problem and try this model. In case they are unable to think of one, have an example ready (e.g., someone takes your turn in a play center, your brother takes one of your toys).

Developed By: Leslie Martin Rainey, Doctoral Candidate, School Counseling

Choices

Grade Level: 3rd
Objective: To identify decisions they make and decisions that others make for them
Time: 30 minutes
Type of Activity: Classroom counseling session (introductory session)
Materials Needed: Drawing paper and crayons, chalkboard
Procedure: Introduce the topic by telling students that today we will be talking about choices and decisions. Then ask students to help you in defining those words. Let them brainstorm definitions. Ask students if they can think of a decision that they had to make in the past day. Let several students give examples. Explain to students that while we are growing up, some decisions are made for us. Others, we make by ourselves. As we get older, most of our decisions are our own.

Using the drawing paper and crayons, ask students to draw a picture representing a choice they get to make all by themselves on one side of the paper. On the other side, draw a picture representing a decision or choice that someone else makes for them (e.g., parent, teacher, etc.).

Let students talk about their pictures. In closing, remind students that more and more of their decisions will be their own. They will need to learn good decision-making skills so the choices they make will be solid ones. Explain that learning good decision-making skills is what the upcoming counseling unit will be about.

Developed By: Leslie Martin Rainey, Doctoral Candidate, School Counseling

Alternative Problem Solving

Grade Level: 5th
Objective: To understand a problem-solving process
Time: 40 minutes
Type of Activity: Classroom session
Materials Needed: Copies of problem situations, chalkboard
Procedure: Introduce the topic by telling students that today we will be talking about problem solving. Most people have problems in their lives on a fairly regular basis. In order to make the best decisions about what to do, it is important to really think through the possibilities. Sometimes we think there is only one way to solve a problem. In fact, there are usually multiple methods of working through a problematic situation. Today we are going to practice using a model to help in problem solving. Read the following scenario:

> Jan and Marcy had been best friends for years. Jan was asked to join a fifth-grade girls' club outside of school; Marcy was not invited. What should Jan do?

Ask students to brainstorm all possibilities of solutions. Write the suggestions on the board no matter how "far out" they may seem. Then ask students to consider the consequences of each possibility. After considering the consequences, have students decide which solution they would select. Explain to students that a simple problem-solving model involves the following components: (a) identify the problem, (b) brainstorm all possible solutions, (c) consider the consequences, (d) make a decision about the best solutions, and (e) implement your decision. Write these on the board.

Divide students into small groups. Read the following scenario:

> Mark and David were in the record store and saw their friend, James, put a tape in his jacket pocket. What should they do?

Ask students to complete Steps 1–4 of the problem-solving model. Tell them that they need to have a recorder in their group who will write down their process and report out to the large group. They will need to give solid reasons for the choice they make. Give the small groups about 5–10 minutes to work together.

In the large group, ask for results to be reported. Encourage students to listen to the solutions and reasoning of the other groups. Ask if anyone would change their opinion after hearing from the other groups.

In closing, remind students that often there are numerous solutions to any problem. As they face problematic situations, they will need to clearly identify the problem, creatively generate solutions, consider the consequences involved with those possibilities, and then make a decision. After implementing the decision, see if it works. With hope, it will. If not, the process can be repeated.

Developed By: Tonya Barlow, MA, School Counseling

Being Responsible for Our World

Grade Level: 8th
Objectives: To learn how to apply problem-solving skills to real-world situations
To learn how to accept responsibility for the decisions made and understand consequences
Time: 40 minutes
Materials Needed: Information sheet on the spotted owl controversy
Procedure: Divide class into small groups of four or five. Distribute information sheet on the spotted owls. Tell the class it is a committee of high-ranking govern-

ment officials trying to decide whether the owls should be allowed to become extinct in order to preserve jobs for the loggers who cut down the forests where the owls live. Review the information sheet and ask if there are any questions. Tell the class it has 20 minutes to make a unanimous decision.

When time is up, ask the groups to share their decisions and ask the following questions:

> What did your group together decide to do?
> How did your group go about making your decision?
> What may be the consequences of your decision?
> Are you satisfied with what could happen as a result of your decision?

Information Sheet:
1. Only a few thousand of the owls are still alive.
2. Experts claim that logging will destroy entire ecosystems and many species.
3. The Forest Service says that a ban on the timber cutting in owls' habitat might cost timber industry jobs and cause lumber and housing prices to rise.
4. Now there is much uncut timber that no one wants.
5. There is evidence indicating that the owls are thriving in second-growth forests that evolve as a result of logging.

Suggestions for Teachers: This lesson may be integrated into an advanced science class when discussing ecosystems.

Developed By: Ann Marie Rice, MA, School Counseling

Making Effective Decisions

Grade Level: 7th
Objective: To understand how decisions made in the past affect the present
Time: 40 minutes
Materials Needed: None

Procedures:	Ask students to write down on a piece of paper their last grade on their report card in language arts. Ask them to think about how they feel now about the grade they received. If they are satisfied with their grade, have them place a circle around their grade. If they are unhappy, ask them to draw a square around it. Ask them to brainstorm at least five decisions they had to make in order to earn their grade. Ask "Did each of these decisions help or harm you?" Place a circle around the ones that helped and a square around the decisions that caused harm. Ask "Do you have more circles or more squares?" Divide up into groups of four or five. Have the groups brainstorm for 5 minutes decisions they must make in order to improve or maintain the grade in language arts. Remind them they should be ones that could be circled. Call time and have them discuss the consequences for each possible decision listed. After 10 minutes, have each student write down which decision he or she needs to make to help achieve a satisfactory grade in language arts in the next reporting period. Discuss the following: How did it feel to listen to others for possible alternatives? Did it help? How did it feel to make that final decision on your own? How can learning to make better decisions help us feel like we *earned* the grade rather than the teacher *gave* us the grade?
Developed By:	Ann Marie Rice, MA, School Counseling

Accepting and Giving Feedback

Grade Levels:	6th–8th
Objective:	To practice giving and accepting compliments and criticism
Time:	30 minutes
Materials Needed:	None
Procedures:	Have students break up into groups of five or six. Arrange each group in a circle with a chair placed

in the center. Ask for a volunteer (A) from each group to sit in the center of the chair. Ask for a different volunteer (B) to start off by giving one compliment about A. Demonstrate by saying something such as, "A, I like the way you always greet me with a smile and a hello first thing in the morning."

Have A respond to B by saying, "Thank you, B."

Next, have B state something that A may want to improve or work on. Demonstrate by saying something such as, "A, I think it would help you in class to come prepared with books and paper every day."

Have A respond to B by saying, "Thank you, B. I appreciate the feedback."

Discuss the following questions:

1. How did it feel receiving compliments? Was it hard for you to simply say, "thank you?"
2. How did it feel to give compliments to others? How do you think the other person felt receiving compliments from you?
3. How did it feel giving constructive criticism to others? How did it feel to receive it?
4. Is it possible for people to give each other feedback without hurting feelings? How?
5. How can learning how to give and receive feedback help us get along better with others?

Developed By: Ann Marie Rice, MA, School Counseling

Conflict Resolution

Grade Level: 10th
Objective: To recognize that solutions to problems cannot always be ideal
Time: 45 minutes
Type of Activity: Classroom session (integrated in social studies)
Materials Needed: Chalkboard
Procedure: This session is designed to be used in conjunction with a social studies class as they are dealing with any war situation. As an introduction, tell students that you will be spending some time with them

discussing compromise and negotiation in conflict resolution. Ask for definitions of those terms. Divide students into groups. Assign each group a particular country's perspective on the war from their text. Give them a few minutes to prepare.

Ask a spokesperson from each group to outline succinctly their country's position. Write those on the board. After all groups have reported, ask if anyone can think of a solution that will meet every country's needs. Usually the answer is "no." Ask students to identify the competing interests that are apparent.

After identifying the competing interests, ask students to consider solutions that might partially serve the best interests of all parties. From the possibilities, attempt to reach a consensus.

In closing, point out to students that this concept of compromise and negotiation in resolving conflict is meaningful in our personal lives, as well as in international situations. Sometimes the solutions to our problems are not ideal, but are the best we can do at a particular point in time.

Developed By: Patricia Maynard, MA, School Counseling

Solving a School Problem

Grade Level: High School
Objectives: To apply a decision-making model to identify a club goal
To apply a decision-making model to determine strategies for addressing a school problem
Time: 45 minutes
Type of Activity: Service club meeting
Materials Needed: Chalkboard
Procedure: This activity is designed to be used with a high school club attempting to address a school problem as their annual service project. Introduce the process by explaining that you are there to facilitate their choice of a project. Ask students to brainstorm problems at the school that might be possible

projects for the club (trash on campus, lack of freshman orientation, library materials, etc.). Write their suggestions on the board. Encourage discussion of the scope of the problem and the likelihood of impacting the particular problem area. Allow students to speak on behalf of the problem they would like to undertake. Attempt to reach consensus. If not by consensus, a majority vote can be used.

After deciding on the project, repeat the process for strategies to solve the problem. Brainstorm possibilities. Consider any consequences or outcomes. Allow students to speak on behalf of plans they think are workable. Again, attempt to reach consensus. If this is not possible, vote to determine the strategies of choice.

In closing, point out to students that they have used a specific and yet simple decision-making model by: (a) identifying a problem, (b) brainstorming possible solutions, (c) considering consequences and outcomes, (d) selecting the best alternatives, and (e) implementing the decision. Remind them that as they implement their decision, they will need to continue to evaluate to make sure the action is working. Encourage them to use this model in their personal lives to make decisions that are solid and in their best interests.

Suggested By: Patricia H. Maynard, MA, School Counseling

Dilemma Discussions

Grade Level: 12th
Objectives: To reason about difficult situations
To hear the reasoning of others related to difficult situations
Time: 45 minutes
Type of Activity: Classroom session
Materials Needed: Copies of the Kohlberg dilemmas presented in Table 8 (see chapter 1)
Procedure: Introduce the discussion by telling students that you will be asking them to consider and make de-

cisions about some difficult situations. Read the Heinz dilemma and facilitate the discussion of reasons for their choices. Discussion can be generated around the following questions:

> Should Heinz have done that?
> Was it actually right or wrong? Why?

Read the second dilemma about Alex. Facilitate discussion around the following questions:

> What are the reasons to tell?
> To not tell?

As homework, ask students to construct a dilemma based on a current social issue, problem for young people, or content from one of their courses (literature and social studies usually provide several possibilities).

In additional class meetings, repeat the process using their dilemmas as "grist for the mill." Remember that in dilemma discussion, the focus is on the rationale—the reasoning process—rather than the specific choice made.

Developed By: Pam Paisley, EdD, Counselor Education

CHAPTER 11

Identity Formation

Introduction

Educators for generations have demonstrated concern for the self-esteem of children and adolescents, and numerous research studies have shown a relationship between self-esteem and academic achievement. However, school programs have failed to show significant impact of this information, particularly in the upper grades. "Time on Task" regulations, concern for Carnegie units, "covering the state-mandated curriculum," and preparing students for end-of-grade tests have reduced the time schools have devoted to these needs. Although schools have given considerable attention to such developmental issues as Erikson's "mastery versus inferiority," they have done little to further the resolution of "identity versus diffusion" and "intimacy versus isolation." Selman's work on perspective taking, representing an important part of the development of children and youth, has had little impact on school programs. As educators struggle with today's emphasis on attempting to plan programs for "at-risk" youth, they would benefit from considering these problems from the standpoint of the relationship between interpersonal understanding and the alienation many at-risk youth experience. If schools are to meet the needs of youth with a variety of cultural experiences, gender differences, family backgrounds, motivation, and learning styles, educators must encourage appropriate progression of children and young people through stages of understanding themselves as separate from others and as being able to relate appropriately to others. Research about school dropouts suggests that the most potent factors that contribute to the decision to graduate from or drop out of school might be subsumed under this topic.

Goals

Children and adolescents will:

- Develop self-awareness and self-acceptance
- Develop a sense of personal responsibility
- Develop a sense of personal power
- Develop a sense of acceptance of human error
- Develop an appreciation for the uniqueness of themselves and others

Sample Objectives

The following are sample objectives by grade level. Each objective is introduced at the earliest possible level, and it is assumed that this objective will continue to be important at higher levels without being repeated in later lists.

K–5 children will demonstrate ability and skills in regard to:

- Describing how they are alike as well as different from others
- Verbalizing a personal trait they like about themselves
- Recognizing that strengths and weaknesses are human characteristics
- Discussing and sharing feelings about self
- Describing what they think is positive about themselves
- Recognizing their abilities to perform specific tasks
- Recognizing that they are important to themselves and others

Middle grade students will demonstrate ability and skills in regard to:

- Learning to accept compliments and criticism
- Identifying unique personality characteristics in themselves and others

- Demonstrating a sense of control and responsibility for personal behavior
- Analyzing their interests, abilities, and aptitudes as components of personal uniqueness
- Demonstrating a sense of control and responsibility for personal behavior

High school students will demonstrate ability and skills in regard to:

- Learning that failure and rejection are not a reflection of their self-worth
- Identifying areas of personal accomplishment and achievement
- Identifying sources of personal strength/limitation
- Learning that their value is not reduced as a result of criticisms or ridicule from others

Sample Lesson Plans

The following lesson plans are designed to provide examples of the types of specific activities that could be incorporated into an ongoing classroom counseling unit or integrated within academic curricula. They are chosen to deal with a particular developmental task or event, or to offer opportunities for growth. However, counselors are encouraged to remember that developmental programs to foster identity development involve long-term interventions to meet K–12 goals and objectives. School-wide interventions such as peer facilitation, special recognition programs, and extracurricular activities can assist in helping students begin to clarify a sense of self.

Similarities and Differences

Grade Level:	2nd
Objective:	To see how students are alike as well as different
Time:	30 minutes
Type of Activity:	One session in a classroom counseling unit
Materials Needed:	List of characteristics
Procedure:	Begin by telling students that we are alike in many ways, but that we are also different in many ways. We are going to look at how we are alike and dif-

ferent today. Develop a list of characteristics (e.g., has blue eyes, likes to draw, is the youngest in the family, hates ice cream). Orally, give the students two of these at a time and let them mingle to see how many people they can find with these characteristics. Bring them back together and let them share. Repeat these with all the other characteristics on the list. After you have finished with all the characteristics and the students have shared, ask the children to tell you what they have learned about themselves or their classmates. What were some of the similarities? What were some of the differences? Are there any other characteristics they have noticed about each other that were not on the list? What are some special things about being different from each other?

Close by telling the students that similarities are special, but that our differences are what make us special and unique.

Developed By:	Tonya Barlow, MA, School Counseling
Resource:	Vernon, A. (1989). *Thinking, feeling, behaving.* Champaign, IL: Research Press.

Who Am I?

Grade Level:	4th
Objective:	To discuss and share feelings about self
Time:	40 minutes
Type of Activity:	Classroom counseling session
Materials Needed:	Paper and pencils
Procedure:	Introduce the activity by telling the students that today we are going to look at who we are. To do this we are going to pretend we have our own personal time machine. We are going to use this time machine to look at ourselves at different times in our life.

Let the students pretend they are going back in the time machine to when they were 5 years old. Have them write down on a piece of paper some ideas about themselves at this age. What were they like?

IDENTITY FORMATION

What did they do for fun? What were their fears? What was their favorite toy? Continue in the time machine to the present. Use some of the same questions or different ones to get students to think about who they are now. Finally, move them into the future. Keep this simple and concrete. What kind of job would they like to have? What kind of family would they like to have? What dreams do they have for their futures? Remind them that these do not have to be definite plans—just dreams or ideas.

After the students have finished the time machine activity, allow them to share their results. What have they learned about themselves? How did they feel about doing this activity? What was hard about it? What was easy? What were some things they liked about themselves in the past, present, and future? What things did they dislike or would like to change?

Close by letting students know how their identity is made up of their past, present, and future. Also remind them that they can change some of the things that they disliked so that they will be happier now and in the future.

Developed By:	Tonya Barlow, MA, School Counseling
Resource:	Kaufman, G., & Raphael, L. (1990). *Stick up for yourself*. Minneapolis, MN: Free Spirit Publishing.

Strengths and Weaknesses

Grade Level:	Kindergarten
Objective:	Recognize that strengths and weaknesses are human characteristics
Time:	30 minutes
Type of Activity:	Classroom counseling session
Materials needed:	Paper, crayons, *Whistle for Willie* by E.J. Keats
Procedure:	Introduce the session by telling students that we all have things that we are good at and can do well and other things that we are not good at. We can learn to do many of the things we can't do now if we practice and take our time. Read *Whistle for*

Willie by E.J. Keats. Discuss the main character's weakness, which is that he cannot whistle for his dog Willie. How did he overcome this weakness? What did he do in the meantime until he learned to whistle? What did he do to learn to whistle? How did he feel when he was finally able to whistle? Let the students share some of the things that they have learned to do and also some of the things they would like to learn to do.

Pass out the materials and have the students draw two pictures. On one side of the paper they should draw a picture of something they have learned to do that they couldn't do before. On the other side, draw a picture of something they cannot do now, but would like to learn to do. Allow them to share their pictures if they would like.

Close the lesson by reminding the students that we all have things we do well and other things that we may not always be able to do as well as we would like. Emphasize that, through practice and hard work, we can learn to do some of the things we can't do or to do better in things we are not good at.

Developed By: Tonya S. Barlow, MA, School Counseling

Unfinished Sentences

Grade Levels: 6th–8th
Objective: To help students explore their personal values, attitudes, and ideas
Time: 30 minutes
Type of Activity: Classroom or small group
Materials Needed: Unfinished sentences
Procedure: This activity is designed to promote self-awareness and understanding and respect within the group. Introduce the purpose and classroom rules such as respecting others and speaking one at a time.

The sentence completions can be gathered from a variety of resources and boundary breaking exercises. A few examples are:

The best thing about me is...
The thing that makes me a good friend is...
I like it when somebody says to me...
When I feel sad I...
Something that bothers me is...
I appreciate/value/believe that...
When people tease me...
Something I do well is...
I can help other people to...
The most powerful/incredible person I know is...
I have difficulty dealing with...
If I were a teacher I would...
If I want to, I can...
When I need help I...
I am proud that I...

Instruct the students to respond to the sentences one at a time and to listen attentively to each other. Arrange the group in a circle so they can see and hear everyone.

The students can select sentences from the list or the adult/teacher can have this role. This will generate endless discussion and writing topics and ideas for further identity-exploration activities.

Developed By: Lisa Murray, MA, School Counseling

On the Walls

Grade Levels: 6th–8th
Objective: To help students develop an appreciation for the uniqueness of self and others.
Time: 30 minutes
Type of Activity: Classroom and bulletin board designing
Materials Needed: Paper, paints, markers, other art supplies, tape, thumb tacks, bulletin boards
Procedure: Introduce this activity as an exploration of the unique qualities of the individuals in this classroom.
Have students spend 2–4 minutes interviewing a partner.

Use questions like: Whom do you live with? What do you do when you are not at school? What do you hope to learn this year?

Briefly introduce partners by giving their name and one new and interesting fact they discovered about them.

Discuss the variety—similarities and differences—among students. Explain that you hope to display these features on the walls and discuss the possible categories of Home/Family, School, Leisure, Favorite Things, Work/Career Directions, and Future Plans and Dreams.

Designate areas for specific topics and have every student make a personal contribution to the visual display.

Students may decide to bring pictures from home or other keepsakes to represent themselves.

Suggestions for
Teachers: Provide time for students to brainstorm and generate ideas, but encourage them to fill the areas according to their interests.

This activity may involve follow-up to allow the students to write, paint, and create their representative pieces.

Developed By: Lisa Murray, MA, School Counseling

The Kids' Book of Questions

Grade Levels: 6th–8th
Objectives: To explore interests, attitudes, and experiences among students
                  To generate ideas for further lessons and promote critical thinking skills
Time: Varied
Type of Activity: Classroom and small group
Materials Needed: *The Kids' Book of Questions* by Gregory Stock (NY: Workman Publishing, 1988).
Procedure: This is an excellent resource for both classroom and small-group sessions. It comes with a teach-

ers' guide that suggests a variety of activities to incorporate into the curriculum.

The questions are thought provoking and stimulating. There are no right answers; the questions provide an easy and playful way to foster self-disclosure and build trust within the group.

If you encourage open and honest discussions, students will be motivated to think, debate, and learn about themselves and their classmates.

The teachers' guide provides terrific suggestions for activities in certain subject areas: public speaking, language arts, art, mathematics, and social studies.

The guide also groups questions according to the subject addressed (e.g., friendship, rules, secrets, self-image, divorce, honesty), which can serve as a quick way to find an appropriate question.

The activities build on the questions by using support materials such as articles, books, and current events to enhance the discussion and many, many creative lesson ideas.

Developed By: Lisa Murray, MA, School Counseling

Creative Self-Expression Activities

Grade Level: 9th (especially appropriate for academically gifted or special education groups)
Objectives: To learn about oneself and others through expressive writing and pictures
To appreciate differences in self-expression
Time: 30–50 minutes
Type of Activity: These activities can be used as a classroom counseling session or a small-group counseling session.
Materials Needed: White drawing paper, colored pencils or crayons, pens or pencils, notebook paper
Procedure: Pass out the drawing paper and crayons before starting the session. Have students get out a couple of sheets of notebook paper, and a pen or pencil.
Inform the students that they are going to be doing creative self-expression activities and that the

activities are not to be graded. Let them know that the session is meant to be enjoyable and a time to express oneself without the pressure of a grade or having to write or draw for someone other than themselves.

If the session is being done by a school counselor, many of the students may not know him or her; therefore, the counselor could have the students say their names and two facts about themselves. This makes the session more personal.

A good opening activity is called "The Scribble." Have the students stand up beside their desk. They may close their eyes or leave them open. Have them imagine they are holding a large crayon in each hand and that they are standing before a large blank white wall. Let them imagine that they are scribbling all over the wall and should try to color all over the space. Ask them to move their arms freely; it is a good idea to participate with the students in this activity.

After this, have the students sit down and scribble all over their sheets of paper with their eyes closed. They may use all of their crayons, choosing any color that they wish. Let them know that they do not have to draw a specific picture. Stop this part of the activity after a few minutes. Now ask the students to examine their scribbles. Ask them if they see certain patterns, pictures, or shapes. Have them outline any patterns or shapes that they see. Also, tell them that they may add things to their scribble if they want. Spend some time having the students share their scribbles. Ask them what they saw in scribbles, about the colors they used, how it felt to scribble, and if anything in the scribble has special meaning to them. An optional step to this activity is to have them write about the scribbling experience using the same topics used to discuss and share. Close the activity by discussing what they may have learned about themselves and others in doing the activity.

Other Options:	A modification of this activity is to play soothing music and have students draw to it. Ask them to draw how the music makes them feel.
Have students draw a picture of what they would do if they had the power to do anything. After, ask them to write a paragraph about it.
Ask students to finish open-ended sentences as they wish. Tell them to write down the first thing that comes to their minds. Suggested sentence stems are: (a) Love is... (b) Hate is... (c) Beauty is... (d) Anxiety is... (e) Freedom is... (f) Fear is... (g) Happiness is... (h) Sadness is... (i) School is... (j) Life is...
All of these activities should involve students sharing their creative expressions. Encourage this during the session. Leave time at the end of the session to discuss how these activities made the students feel. Thank students for their willingness to participate.
Developed By:	Anna Suddreth, MA, School Counseling
Resource:	*Windows to our children* by V. Oaklander (Highland, NY: Center for Gestalt Development, 1988)

Me Collage

Grade Level:	9th or 10th
Objective:	To be able to identify one's own values, likes, and dislikes
Time:	Two sessions (each approximately 1 hour long)
Type of Activity:	This activity is part of a 2-day classroom counseling session. It may be integrated into a teen living or home economics class. In addition, it is a nice small-group activity.
Materials Needed:	Old magazines, glue, poster paper
Procedure:	Have materials placed on students' desks as they arrive. Tell students that this is their collage. Ask students to include pictures of things, words, and sentences that represent themselves. They may be cuttings that describe them in the past, present, or future. They may include pictures of items they value, like, or dislike.

During the first session, students should be given the entire time to work on their collages. Be sure to allow time for cleanup.

During the second session, students should be allowed to finish their collages during the first half. During the second part of this session, facilitation of the sharing of the collages should take place. Ask students to discuss their pictures and their reasons for their selections.

Developed By: Anna C. Suddreth, MA, School Counseling

Who Am I? Book

Grade Levels:	9th and 10th
Objective:	To identify sources of personal strengths and weaknesses
Time:	60–90 minutes
Type of Activity:	This can be used as part of a classroom counseling session on career development.
Materials Needed:	Blank white paper, colored construction paper, crayons, stapler
Procedure:	Tell students that learning about themselves is one of the first steps to take in the career planning process. Ask them to put together a booklet of white pages stapled between two pages of colored construction paper. Ask them to put each of the following headings on a separate page of their book:

> What do I like to do?
> What are my interests? (hobbies, school subjects, activities)
> What is my temperament? My personality?
> What can I do or learn to do?
> What types of people do I want to work with?
> What working environment suits me best?
> What is really important to me in a job?

Tell students to brainstorm and write as much as they can in their books for each section. Also, inform students that they may want to illustrate their books.

Developed By: Anna C. Suddreth, MA, School Counseling

CHAPTER 12

Respect for Self and Others

Introduction

Children and adolescents are extremely vulnerable to criticisms and name calling by peers, presenting something of a paradox for educators who attempt to stop this harmful process. Although each child cares immensely what others think of him or her, often this caring results in joining with the group in ostracizing children who are different in some way. To be accepted, one must reject. Realizing the hurt that comes from rejection rarely carries over into an empathic understanding of how rejection hurts other children. Kohlberg's moral reasoning theory can provide some understanding of this lack of empathy, and it can explain children's need to conform to group norms. Erikson's explanations of the developmental stages, which include identity versus diffusion and intimacy versus isolation, are also helpful. One of the most useful theories is provided by Selman, who identified perspective taking as an important part of growth. School counselors and other educators will find a significant challenge in attempting to bring young people to the realization that our behavior can be hurtful to others and that we can also teach ourselves to reduce the impact of the behavior of others.

Goals

Children and adolescents will:

- Develop self-awareness and self-acceptance
- Develop understanding of and respect for others
- Develop understanding of and respect for persons who differ from themselves in regard to height, weight, gender, race, age, sexual orientation, cultural heritage, and other characteristics
- Develop an understanding of the negative effects of stereotyping and labeling on human interactions
- Develop an understanding of the consequences of prejudice

Sample Objectives

The following are sample objectives by grade level. Each objective is introduced at the earliest possible level, and it is assumed that this objective will continue to be important at higher levels without being repeated in later lists.

K–5 children will demonstrate ability and skills in regard to:

- Describing how they are alike as well as different from others
- Describing what they think is positive about themselves
- Recognizing their abilities to perform specific tasks
- Recognizing that they are important to themselves and others
- Recognizing cultural differences and describing ways to accept those differences
- Learning to make positive statements about themselves and others
- Identifying how others might be feeling
- Recognizing negative effects of teasing others about the way they express feelings (name calling such as "cry baby," etc.)
- Recognizing the effect of "labels" on relationships with others

Middle grade students will demonstrate ability and skills in regard to:

- Accepting compliments and criticism
- Defining stereotyping and identifying negative effects
- Recognizing their characteristics and abilities as well as those of others, and identifying their strengths
- Identifying unique personality characteristics in themselves and others
- Analyzing their interests, abilities, and aptitudes as components of personal uniqueness

- Analyzing effective peer and family relationships, their importance, and how they are formed
- Analyzing how conflict-resolution skills improve relationships with others

High school students will demonstrate ability and skills in regard to:

- Learning that failure and rejection are not a reflection of their self-worth
- Learning ways to access personal strengths and positive self-talk in coping with difficult situations
- Differentiating criticism of "who one is" from "what one does"
- Developing an understanding of how individual contributions impact society
- Examining consequences of prejudice
- Identifying "self put downs" and learning to apply positive self-talk
- Identifying their positive and negative attitudes and developing ways to avoid excess negativity
- Learning ways to value themselves even if others don't treat them as worthwhile people
- Differentiating between "bragging" and sharing positive aspects of themselves
- Recognizing the effect of judgmental attitudes toward others
- Recognizing that people don't always share the same values
- Describing positive qualities of people who are culturally different

Sample Lesson Plans

The following lesson plans are designed to provide examples of the types of specific activities that could be incorporated into an ongoing classroom counseling unit or integrated within academic curricula. They are chosen to deal with a particular developmental task or event, or to offer opportunities for growth. However, counselors are encouraged to remember that developmental programs to foster respect for self and others involve long-term interventions to meet K–12 goals and objectives. School-wide interventions that provide opportunities for different types of students to work together and get to know each other (beyond stereotypes and preconceived notions) will promote development in this area.

Children Around the World Go to School

Grade Levels:	Kindergarten and 1st
Objectives:	To describe how they are alike as well as different from others
	To recognize cultural differences
Time:	30 minutes
Type of Activity:	Classroom session
Materials Needed:	A copy of *This Is the Way We Go to School* by Edith Baer (NY: Scholastic, Inc., 1990), drawing paper, crayons
Procedure:	Introduce the topic by asking students how they got to school that morning (bus, car, bicycle, walked, etc.). Point out that different students used different methods of transportation. Tell them they are going to listen to a story about how students in different states and different countries go to school. Read the book. Let students look for similarities and differences. Go back through the pictures slowly. Let them guess why certain modes of transportation are used (e.g., snowmobiles and helicopters in Siberia). Encourage students to discuss the different environments they see.
	Ask students to draw a picture of how they were transported to school that morning. Allow students to share their pictures. Point out that even in one class there are many ways of getting to school. Ask what all children in the book might have in common.
	This story could also provide an opportunity to do a very basic geography lesson. There is a map in the back of the book that shows where the different children live.
	You may wish to expand on the idea of differences by noting differences in names, clothing, and physical appearances of the children in the pictures.
Developed By:	Terri C. Kearse, MA, School Counselor, Minneapolis Elementary School, Minneapolis, NC

Building a Sense of Self

Grade Level:	3rd
Objectives:	To recognize their abilities to perform certain tasks
	To describe how they are alike as well as different from others
Time:	30 minutes
Type of Activity:	Classroom session
Materials Needed:	A copy of *Jeremy's Decision* by Ardyth Brott and Michael Martchenko (Brooklyn, NY: Kane/Miller Book Publishers, 1990), drawing paper, crayons
Procedure:	Introduce the topic by asking students if they are like their parents (appearance, personality, interests, etc.). Let students discuss similarities and differences. Tell the class that sometimes people expect us to be like our families. Sometimes this will be true and sometimes not. Tell students that they are going to hear two words in the story for today: *conductor* and *paleontologist*. Ask if they know what those people do.
	Read the book. The book is about Jeremy, whose father is a conductor. People are always asking him if he is going to be a conductor like his father. Jeremy loves his father and likes music, but he doesn't want to be a conductor. He doesn't know the answer to the questions. He loves dinosaurs. At the end of the book, Jeremy finally tells someone that he does not want to be a conductor. He wants to be a paleontologist. Jeremy's sister becomes a conductor.
	Ask students for their reactions. (Some parts of the story to bring to the children's attention: Jeremy loves his father very much, but is different from him in some ways. Sometimes children follow in their parents' footsteps; sometimes they do not. Jeremy was very proud of himself when he announced what he wanted to be. People are not alike; we all have different interests, talents, etc.) Ask students if they think they would like the same job as one of their parents or family members.

An additional activity might involve having students draw a picture of something they might like to do when they grow up.

Let students share their pictures and one sentence about what they think they want to do. Emphasize again that we each have different talents and interests. Also emphasize that they will probably change their minds numerous times.

Developed By: Terri Kearse, MA, School Counselor, Minneapolis Elementary School, Minneapolis, NC

Respecting the Decisions of Others

Grade Level: 5th
Objectives: To recognize different values and opinions within their own classroom
To develop skills for accepting those differences
Time: 45 minutes
Type of Activity: Classroom activity (integrated in social studies) or small group
Materials Needed: Two posters labeled *agree* and *disagree*, a list of statements related to a particular topic (in this case, our system of democracy) Examples include:

> The legal age for voting should be lowered to 16.
> People in prison should not be allowed to vote.
> Presidents should only serve one term.
> We should cut the salaries of senators and representatives in order to save money to apply to the deficit.
> Politicians should have a higher standard of moral character and behavior than the average citizen.

Introduce the topic of decision making by asking students to comment on how they make decisions. Do they talk to friends? Do they make lists of pros and cons? Is it easier to make decisions in groups or individually? Point out that our values play a big role in the decisions we make. Ask students for examples.

Ask students to gather in the center of the room. Tape the poster that says *agree* on one side of the room and *disagree* on the other side. The center of the room will be neutral territory. Read each statement to the group. Each student must choose where he or she will stand. Ask a few students from each group to say a sentence or two about why they made that particular choice. Make sure that students from each side of an issue, including the neutral position, get to state an opinion or argument for their point of view. Then allow the students to change positions if they have changed their minds after hearing others' points of view.

Process the activity using the following questions:

> Did anyone's answers surprise you?
>
> Did anyone change his or her mind? How did that feel?
>
> Did any of you find yourselves standing on the opposite side of the room from your best friends or a special group of friends? How did that feel?
>
> Which question did you feel most strongly about? Can you be friends with a person whose opinions don't match yours?
>
> Did you learn anything about someone in the group by listening to his or her answers?

Close the lesson by asking students to tell one thing that they learned about decision making. Summarize by stating that, in understanding another's point of view, we can appreciate and/or accept his or her differences.

Additional Suggestions: This activity can also be used with more general statements, not specifically related to a social studies topic. The topics could reflect dilemmas that students face in their personal lives.

Developed By: Terri Kearse, MA, School Counselor, Minneapolis Elementary School, Minneapolis, NC

Learning to Confront Conflict Early

Grade Level: Middle school
Objectives: To learn that resolving conflict early on is more helpful to relationships with others than waiting too long
To learn ways to confront others early before the conflict situation becomes too stressful
Time: 40 minutes
Materials Needed: Inflated balloon
Procedures: Without the students' knowledge, simulate a conflict situation with the classroom teacher in front of the class. The teacher angrily and loudly begins complaining about the team leader (or other school personnel) who has been taking the teacher for granted all year long. The teacher may also say, "I heard she was talking about me in the teachers' lounge and I am getting tired of it!"
Break from the roles and thank the teacher for his or her participation. Discuss the following questions:

>What happens to relationships when you allow something to continue going on that causes you conflict?
>How do you think [the counselor] felt when [the teacher] was talking about the team leader?
>What could the teacher have done differently?
>What could the counselor have done differently?

>Press an inflated balloon very lightly. Explain that if we confront a person *immediately*—when the conflict first develops—rather than keeping it in or complaining to others about it, as did the teacher, very little force is needed to handle the situation (pull finger away from balloon).
>Yet, if keep it inside without talking it out to the other party (the team leader), anger and resentment will build, adding much more stress to the relationship (press with finger down further toward the center of balloon and quickly release).
>Break into small groups. Ask the participants to

	brainstorm possible conflict situations they may be facing.
Ask students to take turns role-playing each situation.
Developed By:	Ann Marie Rice, MA, School Counseling

I Am Unique

Grade Level:	Middle school
Objectives:	To understand the benefits of being unique
To identify ways in which participants and others are unique
Time:	40 minutes
Materials Needed:	Index cards, a bowl or hat for each small group
Procedures:	Break into small groups. Pass out an index card to each participant. Instruct the students, without putting their names on it, to write "I am unique" on their index card. Tell them to write it any way they choose.
Give a bowl to each group. Instruct each person in the group to place the card in the bowl. Mix up and ask each student in the group to draw one of the cards out of the bowl.
Discuss that even though the cards appear to be the same or say the same thing, they are all different in some ways. Likewise they may all appear different, yet are the same in other ways.
Have each student go around and describe one unique characteristic about each card to the group. What does this teach us about people?
Have students identify to whom their card belongs and write the owner's name on the back of the card. Ask students to write one unique characteristic that describes the person whose name is on card. Send cards clockwise following the same instructions until everyone has listed a characteristic. When students get their own card, they must write a characteristic about themselves that makes them unique.
Discuss the following:

	Can two people really be the same in anything? What can happen in society when we do not acknowledge and accept the differences and unique characteristics in others?
Developed By:	Ann Marie Rice, MA, School Counseling

Stereotyping

Grade Level:	11th
Objectives:	To recognize the effects of stereotyping and prejudice
	To consider strategies for changing prejudicial attitudes
Time:	45 minutes
Type of Activity:	Classroom session (integrated in an English unit)
Materials Needed:	Copies of *To Kill a Mockingbird* by Harper Lee (Philadelphia: Lippincott, 1960)
	A copy of Maya Angelou's inaugural poem
Procedure:	This session would be a part of a more comprehensive unit built around this novel. This particular session would be a facilitated discussion about prejudice and stereotyping.
	Ask students to brainstorm as many examples as possible from the book in which prejudice or stereotyping affected the events or plot line. List these on one side of the chalkboard. Encourage students to discuss how events might have happened differently without the prejudiced attitudes.
	Then ask students to brainstorm examples of prejudice and stereotyping in their own school or community. After generating a list of examples, pose the following questions for students: What can we do to reduce prejudice and stereotyping and its impact? Can an individual make a difference? How?
	Close the class with the inaugural poem by Maya Angelou.
Developed By:	Patricia H. Maynard, MA, School Counseling

RESPECT FOR SELF AND OTHERS

The Breakfast Club

Grade Level: High School
Objective: To recognize the effect of judgmental attitudes
Time: Two to three class periods
Type of Activity: Classroom session
Materials Needed: A copy of the video "The Breakfast Club"
Procedure: During the first class period, show the first 30 minutes of the movie. Stop the video and ask students to write brief personal reactions to each of the characters. Encourage them to be honest in their reactions. If they are unable to complete the reactions, ask that they finish them as homework to be turned in the next day.

On the second day, take up the reaction papers and show the rest of the movie. If additional time is needed to complete the movie, this can be done at the beginning of the third class. Assign a second set of reaction papers about the characters at the end of the movie.

The majority of the third class session should be spent in processing a comparison of the reaction papers and the movie. In particular, focus on how their perceptions/impressions changed from the beginning of the movie to the end, and on how the characters' perceptions of each other changed also. Ask students to share examples of this type of change of perspective in their own lives. In closing, ask students to share anything they learned from the movie, the reaction papers, and/or the discussion.

Developed By: Pam Paisley, EdD, Counselor Education

Positive Self-Talk

Grade Level: High School
Objective: To encourage the use of positive self-talk rather than put downs
Time: 45 minutes
Type of Activity: Classroom session

Materials Needed: Chalkboard
Procedure: Introduce the topic by telling students that today we are going to be talking about the kinds of messages we give ourselves. Do we say things to ourselves that make us feel better about who we are or worse?

Present the following situations and ask students to speculate about what messages "go off" in the individual's head:

> A National Honor Society student makes a 44 on an English test
>
> A young woman musters up her courage to invite a guy to a party; he says he can't go—he's not feeling well
>
> A basketball player misses the last free throw in a tied game

Give students a chance to identify the messages. Then present the RET model: (A) Activating Event, (B) Belief System, (C) Consequence, (D) Dispute, and (E) Effect. Focus particularly on the dispute of irrational and negative self-talk. Use the first situation as an example to show them how to use the model. The student makes 44 on an English test. If he believes that he *has* to get great grades all of the time in order to be worthwhile, he will think the 44 means he is stupid and not worthwhile. He will feel down, maybe even depressed, as a consequence. This is an important area for dispute. What could he say to himself as a dispute or as positive self-talk to handle this differently? Let the class make suggestions. Rather than "I'm stupid. I'm not worthwhile," what else could he try? (Realize he doesn't have to make great grades all of the time. Say, "I did not do well on one test. I need to do better next time. I usually do better than this. It's only one test.")

Let students practice applying the model to the two other situations and share their "disputes" with the class.

Close the class by reminding students that the messages we give ourselves can affect how we feel. Encourage them to pay attention when they are giving too much negative feedback. Instead, try giving positive messages! Emphasize the importance of *practicing* this strategy.

Developed By: Kathy Simmons, MA, School Counseling

CHAPTER 13

Wellness

Introduction

Health programs have been provided in schools for generations; yet statistics suggest that American adults and young people are not hearing, not believing, and/or not applying what they are being told. Why? Dozens of possible reasons might be provided, but none can adequately explain the phenomenon. Americans share a tradition that includes using food for rewards and family connections, using food for consolation, valuing an impossible standard for thinness, evaluating beauty based on body size, failing to consider exercise in the same equation as body size, and measuring dietary success on the basis of pounds lost rather than health of the body. Americans also have a tradition of believing that team sports have more validity than do individual exercise programs, beginning in early childhood, continuing throughout the school years, and progressing through the phenomenon of adult TV sports-watching "couch potatoes." School-based health promotion programs must combine awareness of the developmental stages of children and adolescents with cognitive and affective approaches that help to counteract the negative effects of family, community, and national traditions. This is not an easy proposition.

School counselors need to coordinate their efforts with those of health educators, who are already utilizing knowledge of physical development in their programs. We assume that principles of physical development make a major difference in the expectations of the physical performance of young people, but we must also make certain that similar principles regarding cognitive and emotional processing have a significant impact also. For example, children dealing with mastery versus inferiority issues may have considerable difficulty acknowledging that their body image does not conform to norms approved by peers, or that their physical strength does not compare favorably. Young people who have developed physically more quickly or more slowly than their peers may be embarrassed about their bodies and may be uncomfortable engaging in activities that focus on body functioning. Children who are much taller than their peers may develop poor posture in an attempt to hide their height, or adolescents whose puberty development is advanced or retarded may be uneasy about changing clothes or taking showers in the presence of peers. Young people working through stages involving intimacy and connection with peers are particularly susceptible to embarrassment.

One of the most frustrating aspects of dealing with adolescents is their tendency to believe "it will never happen to me." They often engage in dangerous activities such as experimenting with tobacco, sex, and illegal drugs; driving recklessly; or striving for the darkest tan possible. Although this attitude is quite normal during adolescent developmental stages, adults find it very difficult to convince young people of the relationship between present patterns of eating, exercising, and sunbathing and their future health. Great patience and creativity must be a part of any efforts to teach adolescents to develop healthy life-styles. This is particularly true in programs designed to prevent eating disorders in girls and young women. Young women need to learn that dietary habits developed during youth will have life-long effects on their mental and physical health, and that extreme food deprivation and/or purging during adolescence can affect metabolism so powerfully that they may experience permanent difficulty maintaining a desirable weight.

Goals

Children and adolescents will:

- Understand the importance of good health and safety practices
- Demonstrate good health and safety practices

- Understand information about the effects of nutrition, exercise, sexual practices, and the use of various substances on health
- Learn to evaluate advertising and other societal messages about acceptable sizes and shapes of the human body
- Learn to accept variations in body type without negative reactions
- Understand the interaction of mental, physical, and emotional health
- Learn methods of handling stress effectively

Sample Objectives

The following are sample objectives by grade level. Each objective is introduced at the earliest possible level, and it is assumed that this objective will continue to be important at higher levels without being repeated in later lists.

K–5 children will demonstrate ability and skills in regard to:

- Describing their own appearances and recognizing their own bodies as special
- Demonstrating good health and safety practices
- Learning that everyone's body is special and unique
- Learning that nutrition and exercise choices based on health are more appropriate than those based on opinions of others
- Learning that weight goals are more appropriate when based on health rather than number of pounds gained or lost
- Learning to evaluate advertising and reject harmful advertisements

Middle grade students will demonstrate ability and skills in regard to:

- Understanding what stress means and describing methods for handling stress
- Distinguishing between substances helpful and harmful to physical health
- Identifying positive ways of "taking care" of oneself
- Identifying risk-taking behaviors
- Distinguishing between self-defeating and self-enhancing behaviors
- Recognizing the connection between thoughts, feelings, and behaviors
- Identifying negative consequences of drinking

- Learning assertive behavior in response to peer pressure related to sex, drugs, smoking, and alcohol
- Recognizing risks involved in being sexually active
- Recognizing negative consequences of anorexia and bulimia

High school students will demonstrate ability and skills in regard to:

- Identifying characteristics of depression
- Learning positive methods of dealing with depression
- Learning about the effects of emotions on the body
- Understanding effects of alcohol on driving
- Understanding characteristics of substance abuse
- Understanding the negative effects of smoking
- Understanding physical and emotional characteristics of eating disorders
- Understanding characteristics of healthy eating
- Recognizing the consequences of unprotected sexual activity
- Learning self-enhancing versus self-defeating ways to deal with pressure

Sample Lesson Plans

The following lesson plans are designed to provide examples of the types of specific activities that could be incorporated into an ongoing classroom counseling unit or integrated within academic curricula. They are chosen to deal with a particular developmental task or event, or to offer opportunities for growth. However, counselors are encouraged to remember that developmental programs to promote healthy living involve long-term interventions to meet K–12 goals and objectives. School-wide interventions that encourage healthy choices and discourage unhealthy alternatives will assist in this process (e.g., service clubs can focus on increasing student awareness and encouraging responsible behavior).

Strangers and Safety

Grade Level: 1st
Objective: Demonstrate good health and safety practices
Time: 30 minutes

Type of Activity: Classroom guidance activity
Materials Needed: List of situations where strangers may pose a risk to students
Procedure: Begin by telling the students that you are going to be talking about strangers and how students should deal with strangers in many situations. Discuss who strangers are. Are strangers people you can trust? Discuss various situations where students may need to watch out for strangers (on the phone if their parents are not around, at the door to the house, on the sidewalk, if a stranger should pull up beside them, on the playground, in the mall, etc.). Using these examples, give students a variety of situations where strangers may pose a threat, and ask them how they would deal with that situation. Allow for several responses and compare their effectiveness. Allow the students to role-play the situations, with the leader first playing the stranger so that students will have an example to follow. Let all the students take turns with both parts. As the closing, emphasize to the students the importance of using these skills if they are in a situation with a stranger whom they are unsure about.
Developed By: Tonya Barlow, MA, School Counseling

Junk Food

Grade Level: 3rd
Objective: Learning that nutrition and exercise based on health are more approriate than those bsed on the opinions of others
Time: 40 minutes
Type of Activity: Classroom counseling session
Materials Needed: Junk food labels, magazines, glue, scissors, poster paper
Procedure: Begin the activity by telling the class that it is going to be talking about junk food and its effects on health. Ask the students to name as many junk foods as they can and why they may like those foods. How do these foods affect the body?

Tell the students that they are going to make a "Junk Food Hall of Shame." Hand out the materials and divide the children into groups of four or five. They are to put pictures, food labels, drawings, or slogans that concern junk food on the poster paper. They also can create some characters to put in the "Hall of Shame" such as Sweet Tooth Sue or Cola Charlie. Let them share their posters. Discuss the students' own eating habits and how they could change these eating habits to be more healthy (e.g., eat fruit instead of candy). Also, discuss how the opinions of parents, peers, friends, and so on can affect how students choose to eat. Compare the eating habits of students by letting them share their diets on a typical day. How are these similar to their friends in their class? How much do their friends influence their diet?

Close by emphasizing the importance of choosing healthy foods and not choosing foods because others like them or think you should like them.

Developed By: Tonya Barlow, MA, School Counseling
Reference: Idea for "Junk Hall of Shame" from Zeller, P.K., & Jacobson, M.F. (1987). *Eat, think, and be healthy*. Washington, DC: Center for Science in the Public Interest.

Advertising

Grade Level: 5th
Objective: Learn to evaluate advertisements and reject bad ones
Time: 40 minutes
Type of Activity: Classroom counseling session
Materials Needed: Magazines, scissors, glue, construction paper
Procedure: Begin by discussing how adverstisers try to get consumers to purchase products (glamour, power, money, sports, etc.). How are consumers affected by these ads? As the leader, share some ads that you have seen that depict these ideas.

Hand out the materials and give each student two pieces of construction paper. Instruct them to find ads that use negative or harmful ways to sell their product and glue these on one sheet of the construction paper. On the other sheet, they are to place ads that use more positive ways to sell their product (showing benefits of the product, using regular people rather than glamourous ones, etc.). You may need to discuss the difference between negative and positive. Allow the students to share.

Discuss the posters. Which ads were easier to find? How was it confusing to decide whether an ad was harmful or helpful? How can ads that use images of power and so on to sell products be good? How can you decide whether an ad is harmful? Why is it important to know if an ad is harmful?

If time allows, let the students share their favorite advertisements and evaluate them as helpful or harmful. How have these ads affected them?

Developed By: Tonya Barlow, MA, School Counseling
Reference: Gerne, T.A., & Gerne, P.J. (1986). *Substance abuse prevention activities*. Englewood Cliffs, NJ: Prentice-Hall.

Learning Assertiveness Skills

Grade Level: Middle School
Objectives: To learn how to respond assertively in order to resist negative peer pressure that may result in negative consequences
To give students the opportunity to practice using assertiveness skills
Time: 40 minutes
Materials Needed: Role-play situations
Procedures: Review the differences between assertiveness, aggressiveness, and passiveness. Point out that being assertive is to stand up for what you want without violating the rights of others.

Have students write on an index card a recent situation in which they felt pressure to do something they did not want to do, but did not respond assertively. What were the consequences for giving in?

Collect cards. Choose one situation to use as a demonstration. Discuss the importance of making good decisions to avoid negative consequences. Illustrate the different ways of refusing to "go along" (i.e., positive statements first, acknowledging without agreeing or accepting, humor, not giving a reason, etc.).

Pass out the cards again. Have students break into dyads to brainstorm ways of assertively responding to the situation that would result in positive consequences.

Ask for volunteers to role-play their situation in front of the class. Ask the remainder of the class to observe the actors and write down things they like about the responses and what they would have done differently.

Elicit feedback from the group.

Developed By: Ann Marie Rice, MA, School Counseling

Identifying Risk-Taking Behaviors

Grade Levels: 6th and 7th
Objectives: To learn to identify risks in smoking, sex, alcohol, and other drugs
To understand various ways of handling peer pressure
Time: 40 minutes
Materials Needed: Video: *Your Choice, Our Chance* by Agency for Instructional Technology (Matthews, NC: Film Works, 1989)
Procedures: Share selected parts of video with the students. The video shows students in realistic situations involving drugs and other risk-taking behaviors.

After each freeze point in the video, ask the students, "What would you do?" or "How could you have responded in a way that would be helpful to your physical or mental health?"

Allow students to discuss various ways to resist the pressure.
Ask, "What could the consequences have been [in each case]?"

Developed By: Ann Marie Rice, MA, School Counseling

Understanding Thoughts, Feelings, and Behaviors

Grade Level: Middle School
Objectives: To understand how thoughts, feelings, and behaviors connect to one another
To understand how we can more effectively handle stress and the way we feel if we learn to manage our thoughts and behaviors
Time: 30–40 minutes
Materials Needed: Dilemmas involving sex, alcohol, tobacco, and other drugs; colored index cards with a drawing of a light bulb; index cards of a different color with a drawing of a "happy face"
Procedures: Divide participants into small groups. Have each group decide on a leader. Pass out an index card with a dilemma listed on it to each group. Have them agree on a response that would be helpful, not harmful, to their physical health. Allot 15 minutes to choose and write a response on the back of the index card.

Assign half of the members of each group to list the *thoughts* or things a person would have to tell him or herself to be able to choose the response they did. Ask them to use the light bulb cards to record their answers.

Instruct the remaining half of the group members to list the *feelings* that person may have experienced before and after the decision was made. Ask them to use the "happy face" cards to record their answers.

Instruct the group leaders to describe their groups' situation and state how the groups decided to respond.

Discuss the following questions:

- How did your decision or behavior affect the way you felt? Did you feel better or worse?
- How did your thoughts and self-talk affect your feelings as you were deciding how to respond?

Point out that we can more effectively handle stress and the way we feel if we learn to manage our thoughts and behaviors.

Developed By: Ann Marie Rice, MA, School Counseling

Feelings and Wellness—Related?

Grade Level: 10th
Objectives: To identify and express feelings healthfully
To become aware of the connection between feelings and overall well-being
Time: 1 hour
Type of Activity: Classroom counseling session
Materials Needed: Several prepared situations for the class to discuss, blackboard
Procedure: Ask students to identify as many "feeling" words as they can. List these words on the blackboard.
Ask: How do our feelings affect us (behavior, physically, psychologically)? They can overwhelm us and, depending on how we deal with them, they can negatively impact us both physically and psychologically, as well as in terms of self-defeating behavior.
Ask: Does everyone feel the same way about the same situation (people can feel differently about the same situation and some events can elicit a number of different feelings in the same individual)?
Read several situations (i.e., being stood up, getting a "B" on a test) to the students and ask them to share their feeling responses—does everyone have the same response? (If the class size is adequately small, you can have each student write one situation on a notecard, put all notecards in a "hat,"

have each student draw a card out of the hat, read it, share his or her feeling reaction to it, and then have a short discussion.)

Explain to students that some people try to bury their feelings, run away from them, or ignore them in hopes that they'll go away. When an individual does this often, he or she loses awareness of his or her feelings or even loses trust in his or her own experiences—and they often feel "empty."

Ask: What happens if you don't recognize and express your feelings? They find other outlets for expression (i.e., nervous habits [smoking, overeating], reckless driving, or stress-related illnesses [heart problems, ulcers, cancer]). Some people withdraw, become depressed, or act out for attention.

Ask: How do you become more aware of your feelings? (Pay attention to yourself several times a day and ask yourself how you're feeling at the moment, keep a journal, check to see how your body is responding in terms of stomach- or headaches, muscle tension, etc.) Look carefully at the source of your feelings to see if there's a problem that needs to be solved—do you need to act on it?

As you become more aware of your feelings, learn how to express them in healthy ways (discuss this). How can you express them? (Talk to someone, write/keep a journal, draw, exercise, cry, dance, yell, laugh, sing, etc.)

Summary: Feelings are neither bad nor good, although the ways we chose to express them can be. For better well-being, we need to be aware of our feelings, accept them as being okay, and develop healthy ways of expressing them. We need a full range of emotions, both positive and negative, in order to be fully alive.

Suggestions for Teachers:	English teachers: Have students keep a "Thought" diary to help them be aware of and examine their feelings.
Developed By:	Katharine Simmons, MA, School Counseling

To Stress or Not to Stress?

Grade Levels:	11th and 12th
Objectives:	To increase awareness of stress
	To improve coping mechanisms for stress
Time:	1 hour
Type of Activity:	Classroom counseling session
Materials Needed:	Blackboard
Procedure:	Ask: What is stress (physical/psychological response to perceived demand/danger)?
	Explain that everyone has stress from time to time, but that some individuals experience more stress more often. Mention that some stress may actually be beneficial if it inspires us to accomplish things, but that too much stress or the inability to effectively cope with stress can damage both our physical and mental well-being.
	Explain that "stressors" are found in various parts of our lives: academic and social situations, lifestyle (eating, sleeping, exercise), and environment (conditions around us, i.e., noise).
	Ask the students to give examples of signs of stress and list their responses on the blackboard under the categories of *physical* (increased blood pressure, headaches, neck pains, stomach problems, change in appetite, lack of energy, etc.), *behavioral* (more smoking/nailbiting, poorer concentration, greater difficulty sleeping/sleeping more often, etc.), and *psychological* (feeling "down," frequent mood changes, feeling "uptight," forgetting things, etc.). Discuss the occurrence of these symptoms for class members.
	Give the class several minutes to list their own stressors, then have them share their lists and write their responses on the blackboard.
	Divide the class into groups of five, and have them discuss their strategies for coping with stress (e.g., exercise, talking to others, keeping a journal, adequate sleep, good nutrition, a good scream/cry, laughter, doing something fun, reading a good book, relaxation exercises, setting aside time for your-

self every day, developing a new hobby, watching a movie, working on time management, watching a sunset, saying "no," not owning problems that aren't yours).

Ask the groups to share their coping strategies and discuss these strategies.

Developed By: Katharine Simmons, MA, School Counseling

Test Management

Grade Level: 10th
Objective: To improve test preparation and lessen test anxiety
Time: 50 minutes
Type of Activity: Classroom counseling session
Materials Needed: Blackboard, handout (see Addendum A)
Procedure: Lecture/discussion format

Ask: Has anyone ever walked into a classroom to take a test and felt unprepared for it? Has anyone forgotten everything when a test has been placed in front of them?

There are two bases for these: inadequate preparation and test anxiety.

Why do teachers give tests? (To see if you understand the material you've covered in class.) What must you do in order to understand the material? (The keys are to keep up with assignments, pay attention in class, and review material regularly.) What is the best method of studying? (Discuss with students)

1. Start studying several days before the test.
2. Review your notes.
3. Look over previous tests and handouts to get clues on what to study.
4. Study for no more than 40-minute blocks, with short breaks in between blocks.
5. Re-read chapter summaries, look at chapter headings, and review words in boldface print/italics.
6. Make up questions you think the teacher would ask and then answer them.

How can you lessen test anxiety?
1. Prepare thoroughly and *not* at the last minute.
2. Get plenty of sleep the night before the test and eat well the day of the test.
3. Practice deep breathing/relaxation techniques when you go in a classroom to take a test.
4. Remind yourself that you've studied the best you can, and keep telling yourself that you *know* the material. You've done your best, and that's all anyone can do.
5. If it makes you nervous to hear others reviewing right before the test, discover what you need to do to tune them out.

What can you do to be in a better position to study for future tests/exams after you've gotten the test back?
1. Look for the specific items and the areas you missed on the test—did you study the right things?
2. Correct wrong answers and learn the *right* answers.
3. Review the way you studied to discover your study weaknesses.
4. Ask your teacher for study/review suggestions.

Developed By: Kathy Simmons, MA, School Counseling

Addendum A: Test Preparation Tips

What is the best method of studying?
1. Start studying several days before the test.
2. Review your notes.
3. Look over previous tests and handouts to get clues on what to study.
4. Study for no more than 40-minute blocks, with short breaks in between blocks.
5. Re-read chapter summaries, look at chapter headings, and review words in boldface print/italics.
6. Make up questions you think the teacher would ask and then answer them.

How can you lessen test anxiety?
1. Prepare thoroughly and *not* at the last minute.
2. Get plenty of sleep the night before the test and eat well the day of the test.
3. Practice deep breathing/relaxation techniques when you go in a classroom to take a test.
4. Remind yourself that you've studied the best you can, and keep telling yourself that you *know* the material. You've done your best, and that's all anyone can do.
5. If it makes you nervous to hear others reviewing right before the test, discover what you need to do to tune them out.

What can you do to be in a better position to study for future tests/exams after you've gotten the test back?
1. Look for the specific items and the areas you missed on the test—did you study the right things?
2. Correct wrong answers and learn the *right* answers.
3. Review the way you studied to discover your study weaknesses.
4. Ask your teacher for study/review suggestions.

Will I Ever Get It All Done on Time?

Grade Level:	11th
Objective:	To improve time-management skills
Time:	40 minutes
Type of Activity:	Classroom counseling session
Materials Needed:	None
Procedures:	Lecture/discussion format
	Ask: How many of you wait until the last minute before you start on a project? How many of you have ever felt like you've got so many things to do that you'll never get them all done? What do you do when this happens? The key to avoiding this is time management.
	The first step in time management is to know when all papers are due and when you have tests. It's important to keep all of these dates recorded in a calendar so you won't be surprised. This way you can also schedule time in advance for studying and you won't have to cram at the last minute—this doesn't work—it mostly stresses you out.

How many of you are aware of how you actually spend your time? Most of us waste a lot of hours that could be better spent—either studying or at leisure. Be aware of how you waste your time.

Scheduling is very important. Set priorities—what *has to* be done today and what can realistically be put off until tomorrow? Make a "to do" list both at the beginning of the week and every day—this way you can see what needs to be done today and you'll be able to manage it. Remember to keep your schedule realistic and to reserve time for fun things so you don't get burned out.

Reward yourself for meeting your study goals on time. If you've got a hobby you really enjoy, make a deal with yourself: If (and only if) you get a certain project done on time, then you'll give yourself an extra hour of doing something fun.

Discover your "prime time" for studying: Plan to do homework and study when you're most alert—you'll do better and remember more, and you'll probably finish in less time. It's also more time efficient in terms of hours spent studying for a test if you spend 10 minutes per night reviewing what you did that day, for each of your classes.

Students will generally have many questions about these suggestions, so use the rest of the class time answering them.

Developed By: Katharine Simmons, MA, School Counseling

A Healthy Body Leads to a Healthy Mind

Grade Level: 9th
Objective: To promote better physical and mental health through a healthy life-style
Time: 1 hour
Type of Activity: Classroom counseling session (or incorporated into a home economics/health class)
Materials Needed: None
Procedure: Ask: How do you feel when you've gotten only a few hours of sleep? How do you feel when you

haven't eaten anything all day? Can you function well under these conditions? No.

Everything you do, all of your habits, affect both your body and your mind, and both physical and mental factors contribute to your health.

Goals for good health: (Discuss with the class)

1. Exercise for at least 20 minutes, 3 days per week (this relieves stress, clears your head, improves your cardiovascular system, and typically results in feeling better about yourself, both mentally and physically).
2. Always eat breakfast and never skip meals (a good breakfast helps to start your day off right, gives your muscles the fuel they need, and actually helps you think better).
3. Eat well—low fat, caffeine, and sugar; high fiber; and remember to drink water (water flushes your body of harmful chemicals).
4. Never diet—lose weight through exercise instead of starving yourself. Our bodies adapt to changes in the amount of food we give them. When we starve ourselves, our bodies go into a "shutdown" mode. When we start to eat normally again, it's too much food for our bodies and we gain weight.
5. Don't smoke—it fills up your lungs and hampers your breathing, puts stress on your heart and makes it pump harder, and takes away fun-filled years of your life. If you smoke "to relieve stress," try something else like exercise, talking out your problems, or reading a good book.
6. Get enough sleep—at least 7 or 8 hours each night. Sleep is the way your body recharges itself. When you skimp on sleep, you're short-changing yourself.
7. Take time to have fun—laughter releases chemicals in the body that give us a "natural high." Plan fun activities for yourself.

Ask: How many of you do all of these things? What are some improvements you can make to help you

have a healthier life-style? Discuss students' responses.
Developed By: Katharine Simmons, MA, School Counseling

Dealing with Conflict and Anger

Grade Level: 9th
Objective: To increase awareness of means by which to handle anger and conflict more productively
Time: 1 hour
Type of Activity: Classroom counseling activity
Materials Needed: Blackboard
Procedure: Discussion/activity format
Ask if anyone in the class has ever been in a conflict with someone.
Have you gotten angry? (Yes, we all do sometimes.)
Is it okay to be angry? (Yes, it's everyone's right to feel anger, but it's important to recognize why we're angry, what causes it, and whether we deal with our anger in ways that benefit or hurt us.)
What are some things that make you mad? Why? (Often because we feel hurt or we can't control/change others.)
Do you get more angry at certain people? Why?
How do you handle your anger?
The following are ways that some people deal with anger:
1. Keeping it inside—usually this doesn't work because it lets anger build and we either explode later over something small (and look irrational) or we turn this anger inward and end up feeling sad. This can also cause stomachaches, headaches, etc. (How many of you do this? How does it make your feel?)
2. Taking anger out on others—what does this accomplish? (Usually it hurts someone else/makes them mad.) What's your response when people take their anger out on you? (Most people put up a wall and either get angry or don't listen.) Does taking your anger out on another person

solve anything? (It usually makes everything worse, and often hurtful things that no one means are said.)
3. Keep two things in mind whenever anyone says something that angers you: It's important to stick up for your rights without stepping on the rights of others, and it takes two people to have a fight.
4. Here are some questions to ask yourself—to help you think before you act when you're feeling angry:

    Why am I feeling this way?
    Have I really been wronged?
    What should my response be?
5. Scenario One: (to discuss)

    Let's say that someone just called you stupid. Can anyone suggest a response that might be productive for you? (Suggestion: Well, I don't think of myself as stupid. Have I done anything to you to make you feel this way? This often catches the other person off guard.)
6. Scenario Two: (to discuss)

    You just got tripped in the hall and you don't know whether it was on purpose. What do you say/do?

Developed By: Katharine Simmons, MA, School Counseling

CHAPTER 14

Changes

Introduction

The concept of development is most important for educators who are attempting to understand how children and adolescents adapt to changes and attempting to devise programs to provide educational assistance in the process. It is important to recognize that change is inevitable, and that all people must learn to deal with the effects of change. Even changes that are perceived as positive can create stress and require adaptation.

For example, in dealing with the death of a loved one or a pet, the counselor needs to understand the level of clarity the child has concerning the permanence of death. In dealing with a child's response to parental divorce, adults need to understand the level of the child's understanding of the dynamics; many younger children blame themselves for family dysfunction, believing that "If I had only behaved better, my parents would still love each other." Understanding the developmental level of the young person is crucial in planning programs to help young people deal with changes in their lives. Unfortunately, many adults minimize the significance of such changes as the death of a pet, as well as minimizing the capacity of the child to deal with the death of a grandparent, for example. Often adults fail to realize the impact of their efforts to explain death, using language that they think will comfort the child, yet having the opposite effect.

Telling a child that "God took your father because he wanted him in heaven" might seem comforting to an adult, but the child might interpret it to mean, "God is so selfish that he didn't care enough about me to allow me to keep my father." School counselors can provide valuable assistance to teachers and parents in helping them to understand the developmental level of young people, and they can also provide programs to help children learn a vocabulary to deal with the changes that disrupt their lives.

Goals

Children and adolescents will:

- Demonstrate an ability to share feelings appropriately in dealing with changes in their lives
- Recognize the importance of sharing feelings with people who can help
- Learn ways to access personal strengths in coping with difficult situations
- Recognize the connection between thoughts, feelings, and behaviors
- Learn positive ways to cope with change and loss of relationships
- Recognize change as a constant factor in life

Sample Objectives

The following are sample objectives by grade level. Each objective is introduced at the earliest possible level, and it is assumed that this objective will continue to be important at higher levels without being repeated in later lists.

K–5 children will demonstrate ability and skills in regard to:

- Understanding that everyone experiences many changes
- Understanding that changes happen that we cannot control
- Describing positive ways to deal with anger or stress
- Determining situations that produce unhappy, angry, or anxious feelings and describing how they deal with those feelings
- Recognizing the importance of sharing problems with others who can help

- Developing sensitive ways to express feelings to others
- Learning to identify stressful feelings
- Identifying positive ways of coping with stressful feelings
- Learning that negative feelings don't last forever

Middle grade students will demonstrate ability and skills in regard to:

- Understanding what stress means and describing methods for handling stress
- Evaluating how listening and talking accurately helps to solve problems
- Developing sensitive ways to express feelings to others
- Identifying positive ways of coping with stressful feelings
- Learning that "ups and downs" are characteristic of this stage of development

High school students will demonstrate ability and skills in regard to:

- Differentiating between healthy and unhealthy solutions to problems
- Recognizing that solutions to problems cannot always be ideal
- Learning to put problems in perspective
- Identifying beliefs that might prevent one from asking for help with problems
- Examining how past decisions affect present behavior
- Recognizing the degree of personal control over problems
- Learning ways to access personal strengths and positive self-talk in coping with difficult situations
- Identifying ways to make oneself feel better
- Learning that apprehension about the future is normal for this developmental stage
- Learning positive ways to cope with change and loss of relationships

Sample Lesson Plans

The following lesson plans are designed to provide examples of the types of specific activities that could be incorporated into an ongoing classroom counseling unit or integrated within academic curricula. They are chosen to deal with a particular developmental task or event, or to offer opportunities for growth. However, counselors are encouraged to remember that developmental programs to deal with change and loss involve long-term interventions to meet K–12 goals and objectives. School-wide interventions that provide opportunities for students to deal with difficult situations and transitions can help with increasing coping skills and tolerance.

Coping with Changes Within the Family

Grade Levels:	Kindergarten and 1st
Objectives:	To understand that changes happen that they cannot control
	To recognize the importance of sharing problems with others who can help
	To learn that negative feelings don't last forever
Time:	30 minutes
Type of Activity:	Small-group acitivity (family group)
Materials Needed:	A copy of *The Terrible Thing That Happened At Our House* by Marge Blaine (New York: Scholastic, Inc., 1975)
Procedure:	Introduce the book by asking if anyone has had any big changes in their family lately. What are some of the feelings we have when things change? (fear, sadness, anger, excitement, etc.)
	Tell the children you are going to read them a story about a little girl who experienced a big change in her family.
	Read the book. In the book, the girl's mother goes to work and is no longer available in all the ways she used to be. The girl experiences anger, sadness, loneliness, and so on. Things at home don't go as smoothly anymore, and the girl has to make changes in her own routine—helping with chores, and so on. Finally she has an outburst at dinner and tells them how she feels. They listen to her, give her comfort, and make a plan to help things run more smoothly. At the end of the story, the girl is feeling much better about the new situation. After reading, process the story with the following questions:

What was the "terrible" thing that happened?
How was the girl feeling at the beginning?
Have you ever felt like that?
What did the girl do to get help with her feelings?
How did she feel at the end of the story?

An additional activity involves letting students draw pictures of changes at their houses and how they felt. Allow students to share their pictures and how they are feeling now. Ask the children to brainstorm ways of getting help with negative feelings.

Developed By: Terri C. Kearse, MA, School Counselor, Minneapolis Elementary School, Minneapolis, NC

Changing Families

Grade Level: 2nd or 3rd
Objectives: To identify stressful feelings related to divorce
To identify positive ways of coping with these feelings
Time: 30 minutes
Type of Activity: Small-group activity
Materials Needed: A copy of *Dinosaurs Divorce: A Guide for Changing Families* by Laurene Krasny Brown and Marc Brown (Boston: Little, Brown, 1986), drawing paper, crayons
Procedure: In using this with a family group, begin by asking if they have ever had a divorce in their family. Allow students to share at their level of comfort and need. Clarify any misconceptions about divorce.
Read the book. Although this book is fairly short, it is divided into sections addressing different topics: Why Parents Divorce, What About You?, After The Divorce, Living With One Parent, and so on. Stop after each section and let the students have a chance to comment. On pages 6 and 7 of the book, some excellent pictures of feelings about divorce are shown. Let students name the feelings and discuss any they would like.
The book gives some suggestions for coping with stressful feelings. Read the suggestions again and

let the group come up with other ways of dealing with these feelings.

Give students a sheet of drawing paper and ask them to fold the paper in half. On one side of the paper, let each child draw a picture of how he or she is feeling today about the divorce. On the other side, students can draw a picture of one way of coping with or expressing the feeling. Let each child show his or her picture and make comments.

In closing, talk about how feelings change day to day, or even hour to hour. Ask students to name all the feelings they learned about today. Give an opportunity for children to share freely about anything else they learned during the group.

Developed By: Terri C. Kearse, MA, School Counselor, Minneapolis Elementary School, Minneapolis, NC

Annie Bananie

Grade Level: 3rd
Objective: To understand the feelings associated with loss
Time: 30 minutes
Type of Activity: Classroom session
Materials Needed: A copy of *Annie Bananie* by Leah Komaiko (New York: Harper, 1987)
Procedure: As a way of introducing the story, ask students if they have ever had a friend or someone they cared about move away. How did that feel? Let students share their experiences.

Then say that you are going to tell them a story about a special friendship. Read *Annie Bananie*. The book has wonderful pictures, and it is a great "read aloud book." After reading the story, ask the students how they thought Annie's friend felt.

They will probably say sad. Ask about the good feelings she had at the same time. Besides being a book about the loss of a friend moving away, the book is also a celebration of friendship. If most students have experienced someone moving away, ask them to finish the following stem as a way of closing: I miss my friend (or cousin, etc.) *and* I feel happy when I think about him or her.... If they haven't experienced someone moving away, let them talk about what they like doing with their good friend now. Point out to students that we can have mixed feelings when someone moves—sad that they are gone, but full of very happy memories.

Transition to High School

Grade Level:	8th
Objectives:	To familiarize students with the similarities and differences between middle school and high school
	To assist students in the transition to high school and respond to any questions and anxiety they have
Time:	30 minutes
Type of Activity:	Classroom
Materials Needed:	Paper and pencils, high school handbook
Procedure:	Introduce the session on Transition to High School. Ask how many are looking forward to high school and have questions about life at the high school.

Ask students to write an anonymous question regarding high school (e.g., courses, requirements, rules, privileges, lunch, etc.).

Collect questions and instruct students to get into groups of five to seven people.

Each group is instructed to list as many differences and similarities between middle school and high school. Allow 5 minutes for the groups to compile their lists.

Make a combined list on the board or overhead of the differences mentioned by each group and then the similarities. Ask each group to select a spokesperson to avoid disruptive discussions.

Respond to the list of differences and similarities and address the individual examples. This discussion will cover the various rules, requirements, responsibilities, freedoms, rumors, and resources.

DEVELOPMENTAL SCHOOL COUNSELING PROGRAMS

	Pass the anonymous questions out to students and ask them to stand and read the question aloud and answer it (with assistance).
Suggestions for Teachers:	This is an excellent activity because students will provide the material (i.e., concerns, rumors, questions).
	It is helpful to integrate this session with preregistration and visits to the high school.
Developed By:	Lisa Murray, MA, School Counseling

Dear Abbey

Grade Levels:	6th–8th
Objectives:	To recognize the importance of sharing feelings with people who can help
	To help students identify and talk about feelings, problems, and stress, and to encourage positive peer relationships
Time:	30 minutes
Type of Activity:	Classroom or small group
Materials Needed:	Paper and pencil, "Dear Abbey" example
Procedure:	Introduce yourself and the rules for the class session.
	Read the "Dear Abbey" example that you have prepared. I suggest focusing on an issue or problem that is common with this group (i.e., friendship, peer pressure, stepfamilies).
	Ask students in small groups to generate a list of strategies and advice for this individual. Discuss the different feelings and the stress of middle school life. Help students learn that this is normal, and that "ups and downs" are characteristic of this age. Allow students 8–10 minutes to write a "Dear Abbey" letter about a feeling, problem, stress, or difficult decision in their life with which they want help.
	Collect the anonymous letters and select several to read to the group; facilitate a discussion around the issues raised. You may elect to do this as a small

	group or as partner responses to the individual letters.
Suggestions for Teachers:	This activity captures the students' attention because their lives serve as the subject matter for discussion.
	Encourage and model honesty, risk-taking behavior, and respect with this activity and all discussions.
Developed By:	Lisa Murray, MA, School Counseling

Learning About Loss

Grade Levels:	6th–7th
Objective:	To learn positive ways to cope with change and loss, and to recognize change as a constant factor in life
Time:	30 minutes
Materials Needed:	*Badger's Parting Gifts* by Susan Varley (New York: Lothrop, Lee, & Shepard,1984)
	Gran-Gran's Best Trick by L. Dwight Holden (New York: Imagination Press,1989)
	The Sky Goes On Forever by Molly MacGregor (Dawn House Press,1988)
	The Tenth Good Thing About Barney by Judith Viorst (New York: Aladdin Books,1971)
	The Taste of Spruce Gum by Jacqueline Jackson (Boston: Little, Brown, 1966)
	Goodbye, Chicken Little by Betsy Cromer Byars (New York: Harper & Row, 1979)
	The Big Red Barn by Anne Evelyn Bunting (New York: Harbrace J., 1979)
	Paper and crayons
Procedure:	This session will help students realize that others share the same fears, and it will help them identify positive ways to cope with change and loss in their lives.
	Ask students to listen to the children's book you read and to identify the character's fears. Discuss their own experiences with this fear. Identify the

DEVELOPMENTAL SCHOOL COUNSELING PROGRAMS

ways the character coped with his or her fear. Brainstorm ways of coping with this fear in the future. Introduce the story and read it to the group. Discuss the story and address:

> The character and the subject of his or her fear.
> Times they had this type of experience.
> What they do to help themselves.
> What suggestions or advice they have for others.

Discussion of the story provides opportunities for the students to share how they would feel, think, and act in a similar situation, and compare this with the story character and peers.

Afterward, allow 5 minutes for the class to draw or write about this discussion.

Developed By: Lisa Murray, MA, School Counseling

Loss of a Relationship

Grade Level: High School
Objective: To recognize the feelings associated with the loss of a relationship
Time: 45 minutes
Type of Activity: Class session (integrated in English)
Materials Needed: A copy of the poem "Well, I Have Lost You" by Edna St. Vincent Millay
Procedure: Read the poem "Well, I Have Lost You." The poem is about the loss of romantic love. After reading the poem, ask students to brainstorm as many feelings as they could see or hear in the poem. Ask them to identify the specific words that evoked the feeling. Use the following additional process questions:

- What in your life could cause these feelings?
- What words would you use to name those feelings?
- Are there times that these feelings are expressed destructively? Encourage students to give examples.

- How can you express these feelings in ways that don't hurt you or anyone else?
- What suggestions can you make to someone ending a relationship and to someone who is experiencing the end of a relationship?

Suggested By: Patricia H. Maynard, MA, School Counseling

Tuck Everlasting

Grade Level: High School
Objective: To examine concepts of life, death, change, and choice
Time: Three class periods
Type of Activity: Class session (integrated in an English class)
Materials Needed: A copy of *Tuck Everlasting* by Natalie Babbitt (NY: Farrar, Strauss, Giroux, 1975)
Procedure: Use two class periods for reading the book aloud. This book is a children's book, but it is appropriate from fourth grade to adults. Because of this range, the story is appropriate for almost any level of English in a high school. It is the story of Winnie Foster who runs away to the woods and meets the Tucks. The Tucks have drunk from the spring of eternal life and cannot die. Winnie has to decide if she will drink from the spring. If she chooses to drink, she will remain young, whereas others in her family would age.

The processing of the story could be handled in numerous ways. One is to use the suggested literature process questions:

- What did you notice about the story?
- How did you feel about the story?
- How does it relate to your life or to you?

Another possibility is to use it as a dilemma. Should Winnie drink from the spring? Why or why not? What would you choose?

Adapted From: Sarah Borders, EdS, School Counseling

Moving to the "Other World"

Grade Level:	12th
Objectives:	To give seniors an opportunity to discuss future plans
	To give seniors an opportunity to discuss feelings about the future
Time:	45 minutes
Type of Activity:	Small-group activity
Materials Needed:	None
Procedure:	This activity is designed to be used with seniors in small groups during the spring semester. Groups should not include more than 10–12 students. The rationale is to provide a loosely structured forum for seniors to discuss their plans and feelings.
	Provide an opportunity for students to introduce themselves to make sure that everyone knows everyone else and to ground the group. Use basic open-ended questions to facilitate discussion. Examples include:

- How has your senior year gone?
- How are you feeling about being in your last semester?
- What are your plans for next year?
- How do you feel about moving to the "real world" or at least the "other world"?

In closing, wish students the best in making the transition and pursuing their goals. Make yourself available to them if they have additional concerns.

Developed By: Pam Paisley, EdD, Counselor Education

PART FOUR

SAMPLE K–12 GOALS AND COMPETENCIES

Introduction to Part Four

The following information is provided as a resource for systems attempting to organize comprehensive developmental programs. The goals and competencies are adapted from materials developed by elementary counselors in the Watauga County School System. Additional resources used include the curriculum guide for the Carteret County School System, *Developmental Guidance Program Implementation* (Vernon & Strub, 1991), and the *Elementary and Middle Grades School Counseling Handbook* (Paisley, 1989). The mission and philosophy statements could be adapted to fit the needs of a particular system. The goals are broad and inclusive within the domains. However, the competencies should be considered as *samples* because numerous other items would also be developmentally appropriate within the scope of the goals. *Developmental Guidance Program Implementation* offers a much more extensive set of competencies in these domains. The important consideration, regardless of the particular set of competencies selected, is that as interventions are planned, they meet some identified goal or objective. Developmental school counseling programs are planned and proactive in nature (as much as is humanly possible when dealing with schools, children, adolescents, and adults). Such programs also take into account the particular needs of the school and community.

Mission

The primary mission of the school counseling program is to enhance the educational experience of children and adolescents to promote school success and facilitate the development of fully functioning, contributing members of society.

Philosophy

The school counseling program is a comprehensive, developmental program that is an integral part of the total learning experience for all students. The program includes developmental, preventive, and remedial components to promote skills for living and success in schools. The focus of the counseling program is on the total child or adolescent and recognizes cognitive, affective, social, and physical dimensions. Students can benefit from a proactive school counseling program designed to promote personal-social, educational, and career development. This orientation maximizes student potential to become fully functioning and contributing members of society.

Domains

Three domains of development provide focus for school counseling program goals and competencies: personal-social, educational, and career/vocational. Goals and competencies are outlined across grade levels by domain.

CHAPTER 15

Sample Goals and Competencies

Personal-Social Domain

Goals

- Develop self-awareness and self-acceptance
- Develop a sense of personal responsibility
- Develop effective interpersonal and communication skills
- Learn effective decision-making skills (or to make healthy choices)
- Develop understanding of and respect for others

Competencies

Kindergarten students will be able to:

- Describe how they are alike as well as different from others
- Verbalize a personal trait they like about themselves
- Recognize words that express feelings
- Recognize the importance of self-control
- Understand the importance of good health and safety practices
- Describe their own appearances and recognize their own bodies as special
- Describe people whom they enjoy
- Describe ways they take care of themselves

- Describe things they can do without help
- Describe choices they make at school
- Demonstrate the ability to play together cooperatively

First-grade students will be able to:

- Describe how they are alike as well as different from others
- Verbalize a personal trait or behavior that they like about themselves
- Describe feelings they have in different situations
- Recognize that strengths and weaknesses are human characteristics
- Describe the importance of self-control
- Demonstrate the ability to play and work together cooperatively
- Recognize the importance of good health and safety practices
- Describe responsibilities they have at home and school
- Describe decisions they make by themselves

Second-grade students will be able to:

- Discuss and share feelings about themselves
- Demonstrate the ability to share and work cooperatively on group tasks
- Describe how they take care of their physical health
- Describe what they think is positive about themselves
- Recognize their abilities to perform specific tasks
- Describe the process of making and keeping a friend
- Describe how to be a good listener
- Describe decisions they make and describe those that others make for them

Third-grade students will be able to:

- Discuss and share feelings about themselves
- Demonstrate the ability to share and work cooperatively on group tasks
- Demonstrate good health and safety practices
- Describe themselves accurately to classmates
- Discuss two skills they have
- Describe positive ways to deal with anger or stress
- Recognize that decisions have consequences

- Discuss ways to solve problems with friends
- Demonstrate an awareness of classroom responsibilities

Fourth-grade students will be able to:

- Define and discuss the meaning of self-concept
- Define their responsibilities within the home, school, and community
- Identify good health and safety practices
- Recognize that they are important to themselves and others
- Evaluate how verbal and nonverbal communication affects behavior positively and negatively
- Describe methods that lead to effective cooperation with children and adults

Fifth-grade students will be able to:

- Specify personal characteristics they value
- Determine situations that produce unhappy, angry, or anxious feelings, and describe how they deal with those feelings
- Specify personal characteristics they value in others
- Describe ways to express feelings in a socially acceptable manner
- Recognize cultural differences and describe ways to accept those differences
- Evaluate ways they and others listen and express thoughts and feelings
- Demonstrate an understanding of a decision-making/problem-solving process
- Demonstrate an awareness of the problem-solving model and conflict-resolution strategies
- Demonstrate good health and safety practices

Sixth-grade students will be able to:

- Analyze how their attitudes influence what they do
- Understand what stress means and describe methods for handling stress
- Apply problem-solving skills to conflict situations
- Demonstrate an understanding of nonverbal communication
- Learn to accept compliments and criticism
- Begin to understand physical and emotional changes

- Define peer pressure and relate experiences with peer pressure in their own lives
- Describe how interests, abilities, and attitudes change over time
- Define stereotyping and identify negative effects

Seventh-grade students will be able to:

- Recognize their characteristics and abilities as well as those of others, and identify their strengths
- Discuss ways to organize their time and personal belongings
- Distinguish between substances helpful and harmful to physical health
- Identify unique personality characteristics in themselves and others
- Discuss the responsibilities of students in the school environment
- Analyze the pressure they feel from peers and discuss ways to handle it
- Evaluate how listening and talking accurately helps to solve problems
- Provide examples of how past decisions have affected present actions
- Distinguish between personal wants and needs

Eighth-grade students will be able to:

- Analyze their interests, abilities, and aptitudes as components of personal uniqueness
- Demonstrate knowledge and application of assertiveness skills
- Demonstrate a sense of control and responsibility for personal behavior
- Develop skills to cope with the changes associated with adolescence
- Practice dealing with peer pressure
- Evaluate how responsibility helps them manage their lives
- Analyze effective peer and family relationships, their importance, and how they are formed
- Analyze how conflict-resolution skills improve relationships with others

Ninth-grade students will be able to:

- Demonstrate appropriate social skills in a variety of situations

- Demonstrate an awareness of their own uniqueness
- Use their analysis of their own characteristics to set personal goals
- Practice effective conflict resolution skills
- Refine strategies for dealing with peer pressure

Tenth-grade students will be able to:

- Identify their own values and analyze their impact on personal goals
- Access personal strengths and resources to deal with difficult situations
- Maintain friendships with same-sex and opposite-sex individuals
- Recognize self-defeating and self-enhancing behaviors
- Clarify personal goals
- Demonstrate appropriate social skills and effective conflict-resolution skills in a variety of settings

Eleventh-grade students will be able to:

- Recognize the effects of their actions and perspectives on others
- Maintain appropriate and enhancing relationships with adults and peers
- Demonstrate an ability to take responsibility for their actions
- Recognize positive resources for self-care
- Demonstrate an understanding of the effects of values, interests, and aptitudes on personal goals
- Acknowledge limitations without allowing generalizations about their meaning for self-worth

Twelfth-grade students will be able to:

- Synthesize a realistic and positive self-concept
- Accept responsibility for their choices and actions
- Set personal goals for the future based on their interests, abilities, and values
- Begin to develop an understanding of their connectedness to others
- Use appropriate social skills and conflict-resolution strategies to build meaningful relationships
- Appreciate the diversity of views and experience in the world around them

Educational Domain

Goals

- Learn effective study skills and test-taking strategies
- Develop critical thinking skills
- Identify academic strengths, weaknesses, and individual learning styles
- Develop skill in making educational decisions
- Understand their role in group process
- Develop responsible behaviors within the classroom
- Adjust to the school environment

Competencies

Kindergarten students will be able to:

- Demonstrate knowledge of the rules for participating in group discussion
- Demonstrate the importance of following rules for group discussion
- Demonstrate knowledge of effective listening skills
- Recognize the importance of working together in a group
- Adjust to the school environment
- Recognize the importance of self-control
- Demonstrate an understanding of the importance of good health and safety
- Describe the tools to do their schoolwork

First-grade students will be able to:

- Demonstrate knowledge of the rules for participating in group discussions
- Demonstrate knowledge of the importance of following rules for group discussion
- Demonstrate knowledge of effective listening skills
- Recognize the importance of working together in a group
- Adjust to the school environment
- Recognize the importance of self-control and individual responsibility

- Demonstrate knowledge of the importance of learning
- Describe how they plan to do a school assignment
- Describe their favorite school subject

Second-grade students will be able to:

- Demonstrate the ability to share and work cooperatively on group tasks
- Demonstrate the capacity to follow instructions and complete assignments
- Demonstrate knowledge of the importance of learning
- Demonstrate the ability to work independently
- Describe types of situations that make learning difficult
- Describe some purposes for taking tests

Third-grade students will be able to:

- Demonstrate the ability to share and work cooperatively on group tasks
- Describe the relationship between effort and learning
- Demonstrate the ability to work independently
- Demonstrate the capacity to follow instructions and complete assignments
- Demonstrate the ability to draw conclusions from a variety of sources.
- Describe a goal
- Describe a good learning environment
- Learn how to prepare for testing situations

Fourth-grade students will be able to:

- Describe why listening is important in learning
- Demonstrate the ability to set short-term educational goals
- Recognize that people learn in different ways
- Describe things they can learn about themselves from taking a test
- Define responsible behaviors within the classroom, school, and community
- Distinquish between fact and opinion

Fifth-grade students will be able to:

- Describe how success and failure are a normal part of life and learning
- Discuss the "meaning" of life-long learning
- Recognize the importance of completing assignments
- Identify the importance of learning both in and out of school
- Recognize differences in the way they learn for different subjects, settings, and objectives
- Describe how they prepare for tests

Sixth-grade students will be able to:

- Develop appropriate methods for studying and test taking
- Demonstrate the ability to assert themselves by asking questions
- Describe how to design study areas at home
- Become aware of importance of middle school performance to future educational choices
- Develop a plan for monitoring study time
- Identify what motivates them to perform well
- Identify ways that others learn
- Describe ways to study for different types of tests
- Recognize how attitudes influence learning

Seventh-grade students will be able to:

- Demonstrate the ability to plan their own study time
- Describe what motivates them to perform well
- Demonstrate competency in studying for different types of tests
- Apply appropriate educational decision-making skills
- Recognize individual academic strengths and weaknesses
- Implement effective study and test-taking skills

Eighth-grade students will be able to:

- Evaluate the importance of balancing study time and extracurricular activities
- Develop a tentative 4-year education plan
- Identify and appreciate their individual learning styles, aptitudes, talents, and skills

- Participate in orientation activities and experiences to assist with the educational, social, and affective transition to the high school

Ninth-grade students will be able to:

- Continue to participate in transition activities
- Make appropriate adjustments to the high school environment
- Begin implementation of their 4-year plans
- Complete necessary coursework to achieve promotion to 10th grade
- Recognize the relationship between learning and effort
- Set tentative educational goals

Tenth-grade students will be able to:

- Refine their 4-year plans based on experience
- Complete necessary coursework to achieve promotion to 11th grade
- Recognize and adapt to a variety of teaching styles
- Demonstrate effective study habits and routines
- Demonstrate an acceptance of responsibility for academic work
- Recognize the relationship between goals and learning
- Choose electives consistent with personal and educational goals

Eleventh-grade students will be able to:

- Recognize the requirements for various postsecondary options
- Clarify their remaining coursework to coincide with postsecondary plans
- Use appropriate resources to make educational decisions
- Demonstrate independent and responsible study habits
- Synthesize their own abilities, aptitudes, values, and interests to make appropriate postsecondary choices
- Complete necessary coursework to achieve promotion to 12th grade
- Recognize the connections between education and the job market

Twelfth-grade students will be able to:

- Demonstrate an ability to finalize and complete their 4-year plans
- Complete necessary graduation requirements
- Participate in transition preparation activities
- Appreciate the need for life-long learning
- Accept reponsibility for academic motivation and outcomes

- Understand the necessity to plan for retraining
- Evaluate and refine their future plans
- Develop knowledge of resources available to support life-long learning

Career Domain

Goals

- Become aware of personal characteristics, interests, aptitudes, and skills
- Develop an awareness of and respect for the diversity of the world of work
- Understand the relationship between school performance and future choices
- Develop a positive attitude toward work

Competencies

Kindergarten students will be able to:

- Identify workers in the school setting
- Describe the work of family members
- Describe what they like to do

First-grade students will be able to:

- Describe their likes and dislikes
- Identify workers in various settings
- Identify responsibilities they have at home and at school
- Identify skills they have now that they did not have previously

Second-grade students will be able to:

- Describe skills needed to complete a task at home or at school
- Distinguish which work activities in their school environment are done by specific people
- Recognize the diversity of jobs in various settings

SAMPLE GOALS AND COMPETENCIES

Third-grade students will be able to:

- Define what *future* means
- Recognize and describe the many life roles that people have
- Demonstrate the ability to brainstorm a range of job titles

Fourth-grade students will be able to:

- Imagine what their lives might be like in the future
- Evaluate the importance of various familiar jobs in the community
- Describe workers in terms of work performed
- Identify personal hobbies and leisure activities

Fifth-grade students will be able to:

- Identify ways that familiar jobs contribute to the needs of society
- Compare their interests and skills to familiar jobs
- Compare their personal hobbies and leisure activities to jobs
- Discuss stereotypes associated with certain jobs
- Discuss what is important to them

Sixth-grade students will be able to:

- Identify tentative work interests and skills
- List elements of decision making
- Discuss how their parents' work influences life at home
- Consider the relationship between interests and abilities
- Identify their own personal strengths and weaknesses

Seventh-grade students will be able to:

- Identify tentative career interests and relate them to future planning
- Recognize the connection between school performance and related career plans
- Identify resources for career exploration and information

Eighth-grade students will be able to:

- Identify specific career interests and abilities using the results of assessment instruments

- Consider future career plans in making educational choices
- Describe their present skills, abilities, and interests
- Use resources for career exploration and information

Ninth-grade students will be able to:

- Recognize positive work habits
- Refine their knowledge of their own skills, aptitudes, interests, and values
- Identify general career goals
- Make class selections based on career goals
- Use career reources in goal setting and decision making

Tenth-grade students will be able to:

- Clarify the role of personal values in career choice
- Distinguish educational and skill requirements for areas or careers of interest
- Recognize the effects of job or career choice on other areas of life
- Begin realistic assessment of their potential in various fields
- Develop skills in prioritizing needs related to career planning

Eleventh-grade students will be able to:

- Refine future career goals through synthesis of information concerning self, use of resources, and consultation with others
- Coordinate class selection with career goals
- Identify specific educational requirements necessary to achieve their goals
- Clarify their own values as they relate to work and leisure

Twelfth-grade students will be able to:

- Complete requirements for transition from high school
- Make final commitments to a career plan
- Understand the potential for change in their own interests or values related to work
- Understand the potential for change within the job market
- Understand career development as a life-long process
- Accept responsibility for their own career directions

REFERENCES FOR PART FOUR

Carteret County Counseling Curriculum Guide. Carteret County Schools, Beaufort, NC.

Paisley, P.O. (1989). *Elementary and middle grades school counseling handbook.* Boone, NC: The Hubbard Center, Appalachian State University.

Vernon, A., & Strub, R. (1991). *Developmental guidance program implementation.* Cedar Falls, IA: University of Northern Iowa Press.

Watauga County Schools K–8 Counseling Curriculum Guide. Boone, NC.